Wild Food

Jane Eastoe

Wild Food

*A guide to gathering food
in the wild*

THE NATIONAL TRUST

First published in the United Kingdom in 2008 by
National Trust Books
10 Southcombe Street,
London W14 0RA
An imprint of Anova Books Company Ltd

ISBN 9781905400591

A CIP catalogue for this book is available from the British Library.
10 9 8 7 6 5 4 3 2 1

Reproduction by Mission Productions Ltd, Hong Kong
Printed and bound by WS Bookwell, Finland

This book can be ordered direct from the publisher at the website www.anovabooks.com.
or try your local bookshop. Also available at National Trust shops.

ADVISORY NOTE
Reasonable care has been taken to ensure the accuracy of the information and processes
relating to edible wild plants, fungi, seafood and roadkill contained within this book
however the information contained herein is of general interest and in no way replaces
professional advice as to the relative safety of eating such foods. If you have any doubts
whatsoever about your identification of wild plants or fungi, or whether any wild animal
is fit for human consumption, do not eat it.

Neither the author, the publishers nor the National Trust make any warranties as to
the safety or legality of consuming any wild foods. Any liability for inaccuracies or errors
relating to the material contained within the book is expressly excluded to the fullest
extent permitted by law. Reasonable care has been taken to ensure that information
relating to laws and regulations reflects the general state of the law as understood by the
author at the time of going to press. The author, publishers and National Trust make no
warranties as to the accuracy of this information and exclude liability to the fullest extent
of the law for any consequences resulting from reliance upon it.

CONTENTS

INTRODUCTION

In our frenetic modern lives growing your own is, for many, a distant fantasy that simply cannot, despite best intentions, always be realised. Supermarkets are open 24 hours a day and seven days a week, their shelves groaning with produce that makes a mockery of the concept of seasonal food. Piling the trolley high simply does not fulfil our most basic hunter-gatherer instincts – though of course it does perform that essential task of allowing us to feed the family – and we are becoming, quite literally, totally distant from our food source, often many thousands of air miles distant.

It turns shopping into a somewhat guilty experience for the conscientious buyer. Are those delicious plump, red strawberries English, or have they been flown in from Portugal? Is cauliflower seasonal in August? Should I buy another bag of ultra-convenient washed salad greens when I know there are already two mouldering in the recesses of the refrigerator, way past their best-by date? Why do I have to buy jam when my mother managed to make it?

Apart from trying to buy food locally and seasonally, or throwing ourselves into full-time fruit and vegetable production with a couple of pigs and a few chickens, it is very hard to keep in touch with our natural food sources.

In fact most of us are overlooking a wonderful food supply, one that satisfies us personally and, in a very small way, benefits us financially: the wild larder. We have become so out of touch with food that we no longer recognise wild food as something we can utilise. If it isn't shrink wrapped and in a protective plastic container then how can we be sure it is safe to eat? I am not suggesting that gathering some wild greens, or picking fruit, nuts or fungi is in any way going to make you fully self-sufficient, or completely replace the weekly trip to the supermarket. What it does do is put you back in touch with nature and introduce you to new tastes. It allows you, for once, to have a glut of food that can be used creatively.

THE WILD LARDER

Do many people buy fruit from the supermarket to make jams or jellies? No, jam and jelly making is all about utilising nature's excess and you only get that when you grow your own or collect from the wild.

I have to confess to a parsimonious streak that utterly delights in the concept of getting food for free. It is a frankly naughty pleasure, as though I have stolen something. I always feel furtive as I waddle along, pockets heavy with wild plums or bullace, or drift by with armfuls of elderflower or elderberries. It is so rare in this day and age to get something for nothing that it feels forbidden.

Similarly I am exasperated by the wicked waste of all this delicious food when it is left to rot: piles of cob nuts on the forest floor, damsons scattered all over the road, bank upon bank of celery-flavoured Alexanders that remains untouched by human hand. So much food going to waste – and why?

Gathering wild flowers, leaves and fruits is not the sole preserve of the country dweller. We all have days out to the country, annual holidays, visits to relatives: you can use these occasions to gather what you can and you will be reliant on nature and season to provide. Moreover many urban footpaths, churchyards and even gardens are mini nature reserves, packed with wild flowers and fruit if you did but realise it.

We have lost so much of the knowledge that our forebears took for granted. For instance, there are many plant leaves that can be collected and added to salads or cooked as a vegetable. Common garden weeds such as nettles, ground elder and chickweed are all delicious and nutritious – and you certainly don't have to live in the countryside to find them. We regard many plants as poisonous and view any seed or berry with suspicion, but we aren't always sure of the facts. Are the seeds of the yellow laburnum flower poisonous? What about the red berries of the yew? In fact, all parts of the laburnum are poisonous, seeds, flowers, the lot, and all parts of the yew are poisonous *except* the sweet and succulent red aril – the red fleshy bit of the berry – which is completely toxin free (the seeds within it are poisonous however and should be removed before eating).

We hunt for crabs and cockles and examine seaweed on the beach, but do we ever do anything with them – or do we then go and buy some from a local fish market? What about the fungi we all see, sometimes in the garden, often in woods. Why do so many of us walk past without ever taking one or two home for dinner? Mostly it is fear; we don't recognise the weed, fungi or berry, or know whether or not that dead pheasant in the road is safe to eat. All of which can be easily rectified.

I enjoy teaching my children what is what and putting their small hands to good use. A child who has never had fingers stained purple-black from picking blackberries has missed one of life's great experiences. There is something about the process that lodges in childhood brains and is dredged up as an idyllic memory of long summer days. Equally, however, I treasure time alone collecting. The perfect repetition of gathering wild food allows the mind to relax – you can't fret about household chores, work or make 'to do' lists when hunting and gathering.

THE GOURMET GATHERERS

In France a car will suddenly grind to a halt on a country lane and its fabulously chic occupant will hop out, pick a little of this and that, before continuing on his or her journey. Gathering wild food is certainly not the sole preserve of the yokel, although many delicacies, such as the prohibitively expensive truffles currently enjoyed by gourmets and the well heeled, were once regarded as peasant food. Nowadays professional foragers service some of the best London restaurants, providing wild mushrooms, wild herbs and greens like the wonderful sea beet.

True gourmets are learning that, if they want to expand their repertoire, wild food is the way forward. If dinner-party food to impress is what you are after, then wild food gathered with your own fair hands takes some beating!

Elizabeth David, in her book *An Omelette and a Glass of Wine* observes: 'Pale apricot-coloured chanterelle mushrooms from sodden Surrey woods have only to be washed and washed and washed until all the grit has gone, every scrap, and cooked instantly before the bloom and that extraordinary, delicate, almost flower-like scent have faded'.

Novelist and playwright Susan Hill sums up the joy of preserving in her book *The Magic Apple Tree*: 'I make a lot of bramble jelly (which needs some lemon juice to set it or else you get bramble syrup – though that is very nice, too, poured over ice-cream or pies), and then some bramble and apple purée, for the freezer, and then I strip elderberries off their stalk with a fork and make those into a jelly, with apple and some blackberries. Elderberries are an underrated hedgerow fruit, loved by the birds, but very little picked by people, except for winemaking. They have a peculiar flavour and a little goes a long way but it is worth acquiring a taste for and the colour of the jelly and jam is wonderful, a dark, ruby red.

'At the end of this day, I am stung, scratched, sore and stained, and the kitchen smells marvellous. There are rows of glowing jars on the dresser shelves, like so many jewels, deep red, orange, burgundy, pale pink, pale green, purple-black. I label them before carrying them upstairs to the store cupboard, which is in our bedroom, and there, when I have lined them up, I gaze in deep satisfaction, I feel as if we shall indeed be 'preserved' against the ravages of this coming winter, and go off to have a long, hot, soothing bath.'

THE LAW

While the wasteful excess of so much wild food left to rot drives me to distraction, I must also point out that we must all respect the law, codes of conduct and local byelaws, including those of the National Trust, when gathering or collecting. I have not included any rare plants in this book. Some flowers like the primrose or the cowslip were once commonly used to make wine or cake decorations, but are now rarely seen and must be left to seed and spread. Whatever you are picking, don't remove too much at any one time – leave some for other wild-food enthusiasts, although blackberries may well be the exception to this rule as they ripen and spoil so quickly. It is worth familiarising yourself with the Wildlife and Countryside Act (WCA) and Countryside and Rights of Way Act (CROW), which is devoted to such thorny issues as rights of way and public access and the conservation of protected species. If private land has rights of way through it, you may not pick any cultivated fruits and vegetables therein, but you can pick wild plants and fruits – as long as they are for your own use and are not sold – though if you remove a whole plant, roots and all, then that does qualify as theft. You are not allowed to harvest any plants at all from land protected by CROW. Some plant species are protected and picking, selling or destroying them is an offence. For further information on WCA and CROW please look at the list of Useful Organisations on page 91.

Similarly, for fairly obvious reasons, you are not allowed to collect any road kill that you have run over – you can only collect something that someone else has killed. Dead animals found on private land are the property of the landowner. Many wild birds have protected status and arguably you could be prosecuted if found in possession of one – even if you didn't kill it yourself.

You must also use common sense when collecting wild food: don't gather anything from the sides of busy roads as it may well be polluted; fungi in particular absorb a lot of toxins. Similarly don't pick anything from low down at the front of footpaths as passing dogs may well have been happily watering them for months! Take care when collecting seafood that there are no effluent pipes nearby; better not to take the risk and to hunt afresh a little further away.

These practical realities may not sound very pleasant, but please don't let them put you off discovering the delights of nature's natural larder. Fruit, nuts and herbs are natural starting points, but don't stop there; once you've started exploring the tasty green leaves on your doorstep it becomes hard to stop. You'll become braver about maximising the food that nature, not the supermarket, is offering. Maybe next time you come across a dead pheasant in the road you won't drive around it – you'll take it home for a fabulous dinner and you will be very, very pleased and proud of yourself! Food just doesn't come more natural than this – so get back to your roots, get out there and hunt and gather.

FRUIT

Fruit is the one form of wild food that most people will collect with confidence, although if the abundance of fruit going to waste near me is anything to go by it is a pastime that has become less popular. As a child I used to come home with large bags of blackberries unbidden, but children are not allowed to roam so freely today. Yet fruit is the one form of wild-food collecting that children relish – you can guarantee that they will consume quantities as they go. It is vital that adults make time to introduce them to this tantalising natural food source.

Fruit makes a significant contribution to a properly balanced diet: it contains a range of vitamins, minerals and dietary fibre, dependent on variety, and is essential to good health.

There are a few varieties of delicious berries that I have not covered here, for they tend to grow in very specific locations. Cloudberries (*Rubus chamaemorus*), wine berries (*Rubus phoenicolasius*) and dewberries (*Rubus caesius*) are all delicious, if you can find them. They all have the look of a strange-coloured raspberry or blackberry – if in doubt, try one! Mulberries (*Morus nigra*) are also wonderful if you are fortunate to come across a fruiting tree.

PRESERVING FRUIT

Jams and jellies are two of the nicest forms of preserved fruit. Jam needs little explanation, but all kinds of interesting jellies can be made from wild fruit to accompany meat. I should confess that preserving is something of a passion of mine, those little jewel-coloured jars lined up on the shelves never cease to delight me.

The principle is simple: select a mixture of ripe and slightly under-ripe fruit for your jam. Never use fruit that is over-ripe as it will have little pectin content, and pectin is the essential ingredient that makes the mixture set. Then remove stems, cores and stones – though don't bother with damsons, just let the stones float to the top during cooking and then use a slatted spoon to pull them out.

The next stage is to soften the fruit with cooking. Very juicy fruit such as blackberries require very little water, just four or five tablespoons to start the process off. However, fruits such as wild plums need half their weight added in water. Bring the fruit to the boil and simmer until it is a beautiful pulp.

ADDING PECTIN

It is at this point that you may need to add pectin to your mix. There is a test you can do to establish whether or not your mix has sufficient pectin, but life is so short and the test so complex that my feeling is I'd rather eat sloppy jam. Simply remember that fruits such as lemons, cooking apples and redcurrants are naturally high in pectin and are often added to other fruit to boost the pectin content. Blackberries, cherries, raspberries and strawberries have a low pectin content and just won't set without assistance. You can buy commercial pectin, but I believe it is preferable to add a mix of fruit to do the job instead. Lemon juice is used with fruit that loses its acid content on cooking; this includes blackberries, strawberries, sweet cherries and raspberries.

The amount of sugar added to the fruit depends on the pectin content. Fruit that is high in pectin needs to have one and a half times its weight added in sugar: fruit that is low in pectin should have an equal weight of sugar to fruit. Before the sugar is stirred into the mix, gently warm it in a bowl in the oven, to avoid lowering the temperature of the fruit when it is added.

Add the warmed sugar to the fruit and cook on a gentle heat, stirring continuously, until all the sugar has disappeared, which always takes longer than you might expect. When the sugar is completely dissolved and no granules can be seen, turn the heat up and bring the mixture to the boil until setting point has been reached – this can take anything from five to 20 minutes.

TESTING FOR SET

The easy way to test if jam has set is to put a few saucers in the refrigerator to chill. Pull them out one at a time, drop a little jam on to the saucer and let it cool for a minute – if the surface wrinkles when you push it with your finger the jam is ready.

Take your pre-warmed, clean jam jars out of the oven and pour the jam into them. Cover immediately with wax discs and put a circle of cellophane over the top and a rubber band around the neck of the jar. This will form an airtight seal and will stop the jam from going mouldy before it is opened. If jam fails to set and you want to rectify the problem you can always pour the mix back into a pan, reheat gently and then boil hard for a little longer. You will have to clean and heat your jam jars afresh though.

Jelly is made in much the same way, the main difference being that at the end of the process the mix is sieved to remove pips, pulp, stalks and so on. Cooking apples are often added to help setting. When the mix is ready to be potted, tie a muslin square over the top of a sieve and pour the mixture through it into a large, clean and warmed container (preferably one with a spout) and then rapidly on into pots. You have to work fast because the mix starts to set very quickly. Now seal as with jam. It always makes a horrible mess, but it really is worth it.

BILBERRY (*Vaccinium myrtillus*)

The bilberry is a truly delicious fruit if you can find a local supply. The berries are very tasty raw but, if you can find enough, they are even better in pies and preserves. They are also packed with vitamin C so are very good for you and have the advantage of freezing beautifully.

DESCRIPTION: The bilberry is a small, evergreen shrub with distinctive green twigs. The small, bright green, oval leaves have a toothed margin and the fruit is a dark blue black with a whitish bloom.

SEASON: The fruit can be found from July to September; hunt low on the plant and look under the leaves.

WHERE TO FIND: Bilberries like acid soil so they thrive on heaths, moors and woods, notably so in Wales and the north and west of Britain.

BLACKBERRY (*Rubus fruticosus*)

Blackberries or brambles need little introduction as they are probably the best known of all wild foods. The berries are pleasantly tart and are probably at their most delicious mixed with other fruit in a dessert, apple being the classic partner. There are around 2,000 micro-species, which goes some way to explaining why some bushes produce delicious fruit, while others offer only hard and sour berries – make a mental note to return when you come across a delicious supply. Blackberries turn pies, crumbles and summer puddings a deep and dramatic red. Bramble jelly is my family's favourite preserve. It is seasonal and does not keep well, so make just enough for your needs – we can usually stretch our supply to Christmas and it helps if you keep opened jars in the refrigerator.

DESCRIPTION: This untidy, prickly, deciduous shrub can grow to up to 3m (10ft) tall: it produces arching stems and the tip of these fruiting stems send out roots where they touch the ground. Flowers are flushed white with pink and appear from May to September.

SEASON: The fruit forms from July to October and is initially green, before ripening to a deep purple black. It does not keep well, so pick and use as soon as possible, although it freezes beautifully. The berries bruise easily so treat them gently and wash them as little as possible.

WHERE TO FIND: Blackberries proliferate when they are left well alone and thrive on patches of waste ground, in neglected sunny hedgerows. They are often found in churchyards where they were originally planted to keep sheep out.

450g (1lb) of blackberries
450g (1lb) of sugar
Juice of one lemon

Wash the blackberries if necessary and cook gently in 175ml (6fl oz) of water for 30 minutes. Mash the berries to extract as much juice as possible and then add the sugar and the lemon juice. Cook on a gentle heat until the sugar is completely dissolved; do not rush this stage. Next turn the heat up and boil rapidly for about 15 minutes, stirring at intervals. Meanwhile warm your clean jam jars in the oven. When the fruit is cooked pour it through a sieve lined with muslin to strain out all the pulp, decant into a jug and straight away pour into jam jars. If the mixture doesn't set, pop it back in the pan and boil for another 10 minutes. Cover the top of the jam with wax discs and allow to cool before covering the jars

BLACKTHORN, SLOE (*Prunus spinosa*)

This shrub is indigenous to Europe, North Africa and Asia and is much in evidence in the countryside where its sharp thorns and hard wood make it a useful hedging plant. In Ireland the blackthorn was used to fashion the stout cudgels known as *shillelaghs*. In traditional hedgerows it is usually mixed in with hawthorn, holly and the wild rose. The fruit are not that easy to spot if you don't know where to look, which is why the key to successful hunting is to track the plants down when in bloom in late winter and note the location for future reference. If you don't know whether or not you are looking at a damson or a sloe just taste it – the fruit has a uniquely strong astringent flavour. Sloe jelly makes a good accompaniment to rich meat.

DESCRIPTION: The blackthorn is a deciduous shrub or small tree; it has dark wood and sharp thorns. It bears clusters of tiny white flowers in the spring before its oval leaves appear and it is one of the first trees to flower. See below and colour section for illustration.

SEASON: Pick the blue-black fruit after the first frost in autumn (purists claim it is best after the first frost has hit). Wear gloves to pick them if you want to avoid getting pricked by the thorns.

WHERE TO FIND: Sloes can be found in hedgerows and woods throughout the country.

450g (1lb) of sloes
75–110g (3–4oz) of golden granulated sugar
Few drops of almond essence
900ml (1¼ pints) of gin

My father made this every year, though my mother always
used to complain about her gin supply being eroded. Clean
the sloes and remove their stalks. Next prick them all over
with a fork and put them in a large container with the sugar,
almond essence and the gin. Leave in a cool, dark place for
three months, shaking occasionally. Now strain through a
layer of muslin until clear and decant into bottles. If you make
it in mid October it will be ready for Christmas, but it does
improve with age, so keep it longer if you can.

BULLACE AND WILD PLUM (*Prunus institia*)

Of all the leaves, fruits and roots that can be foraged the bullace, a damson-like fruit, is my absolute favourite, but the wild plum comes a very close second. Wild plums are to my mind superior to their cultivated cousins; the flesh is firmer and the taste more subtle. I cannot be trusted to walk alone in the countryside from August onwards without returning with every pocket bulging. I collect the fruit like a creature possessed and throw them into pies and crumbles, along with apples, or make endless pots of pinkish red jam (which I inevitably burn). However, the taste of the preserve is just about the most blissful thing on toast at breakfast – a pure taste of the English countryside. I think it is the shameful waste of this fruit that propels me into a collecting frenzy – for you cannot drive along a country lane in south-east Kent without crushing pounds of the fruit under your tyres. There is a glut of bullace – get out and harvest it and help to share my seasonal burden.

DESCRIPTION: A small deciduous tree with small, hairy, toothed oval leaves. The white flowers have five petals and appear in clusters of two or three. The small blue-black fruit has a greyish waxy bloom. The cultivated damson is derived from the bullace.

SEASON: The blue-black fruit ripens in August and September.

WHERE TO FIND: Bullace can be found in hedgerows and woods, often close to orchards.

DOG ROSE (*Rosa canina*)

Rose hips have been a food source for thousands of years; the seeds have been found in the remains of a Neolithic woman unearthed in Britain. The rose hips are highly nutritious, containing vitamins B and E and more vitamin C than any other fruit and vegetable – 20 times more than the equivalent weight of oranges. During World War II a national campaign urged volunteers to collect hundreds of tons of rose hips to be processed into syrup to keep the nation's children healthy. Rose petals can be used to make rosewater and syrups for flavouring ices and desserts. The Turks use rosewater to flavour Turkish Delight and rose flavouring is also used widely in Algeria, Morocco and Tunisia. Petals can be used in fruit drinks, wine jellies and jam. They can be candied or crystallised for decorating cakes. Both petals and hips can be used to make tea.

DESCRIPTION: The dog rose is a deciduous shrub, indigenous to Europe and North Africa. It produces leaves on arching stems in April; and pretty, five-petalled, pale pink and white flowers from May to July followed by bright orange-red hips. Children make itching powder from hips – the hairs lining the hips and attached to the seed are irritants. If you want to grow a dog rose from seed, leave the hip to mature in the open air before sowing in a pot in late autumn. See right and colour section for illustration.

SEASON: Rosehips begin to ripen from August onwards; gather them when ripe after the first frost – although if the birds are having too good a go at them you may have to pick them sooner.

WHERE TO FIND: This plant is very efficient at reproducing and is commonly found in hedgerows.

EILEEN'S ROSE-HIP SYRUP

900g (2lb) of ripe rose hips
450g (1lb) granulated sugar

This is my mother's recipe. I used to love this as a child, but it is very sweet; if you prefer a sharper flavour, halve the amount of sugar. The mixture will make around 570ml (1 pint) of syrup. Store it in several small bottles rather than one large one, as the syrup does not keep long once the bottle has been opened. Place clean bottles in a warm oven to warm. Wash the rose hips and remove the stalks and calyces then chop the hips coarsely in a food processor. Bring 2.3 litres (4 pints) of water to the boil and add the chopped hips. Return to the boil then remove from the heat and leave to stand for 15 minutes. Strain through a piece of muslin, squeezing the pulp to extract as much juice as possible. It is important to do this straining process properly; the prickly seeds can be a mild irritant if not removed.

Return the pulp to the pan and add another litre (2 pints) water. Bring to the boil then remove from the heat and leave to stand for 10 minutes before repeating the straining process. Transfer both quantities of strained liquid to a pan and boil until reduced to around a litre (2 pints).

Stir in the sugar until dissolved, return to the boil and continue to boil for 5 minutes. Pour the syrup into the warmed bottles and seal. I can't advise how long the syrup lasts – seemingly forever at home, but my mother's kitchen was no stranger to a little mould and mildew! I lovingly made some rose-hip syrup for my children but they were less partial to it than I and the bottle stayed at the back of the refridgerator for months until I finished it off.

ROSE-PETAL JELLY

900g (2lb) of cooking apples
Juice of half a lemon
50g (2oz) of dog-rose petals
Sugar

Wash and roughly chop the apples and place in a pan along with 570ml (1 pint) water and the lemon juice. Bring to the boil and simmer gently until soft and pulpy; strain through a muslin-lined sieve. Rinse the rose petals, remove the base of each petal and dry them on absorbent kitchen paper. Put two teaspoons of sugar into a bowl, add the rose petals and pound until broken up. Place in a saucepan with 150ml (¼ pint) of water and simmer for 15 minutes. Once again strain through the muslin and add to the strained apple-juice mixture. Measure the total amount of liquid and add 450g of sugar to every 570ml of liquid mixture (1lb of sugar to one pint). Bring to the boil and simmer gently until the sugar is dissolved, then boil rapidly until setting point is reached.

JUNIPER (*Juniperus communis*)

Juniper berries are used for flavouring, best known for their contribution to the distinctive taste of gin. They make a very good accompaniment to game and pork in the form of jelly. You can also simply give meat a rub over with the berries as you might with a garlic clove. I like to drop a few berries in with cabbage whenever I cook it.

Only pick juniper berries if there are a lot of bushes (over 100), as this is a priority species under the UK government's Biodiversity Action Plan.

DESCRIPTION: Juniper is an evergreen shrub which carries needles in whorls. The berries start off green and ripen to a blue-black.

SEASON: The fruit ripens in September and October, though it may have taken two to three years to do so.

WHERE TO FIND: Juniper thrives on chalky or lime soils and is most commonly found in the south-east and north of England.

Mesembryanthemum (*Carpobrotus edulis*)

I have a great weakness for these lurid-coloured little daisies. My father cleared an area in our garden for me to have as my own pocket-sized plot and he bought mesembryanthemum to start me off, rightly reckoning that the cheerful little flowers would appeal to the garish tastes of a five year old. These sturdy plants thrived despite my fumbling first attempts at gardening and I was introduced by my father to the delights of their small, fig-like fruit. These are quite juicy and tart, but are delicious stewed – with sugar, of course. It's not easy to gather very many and you will have to fight the slugs and snails for them, but they add an interesting piquancy when mixed with other stewed fruit.

DESCRIPTION: This prostrate plant has woody stems and succulent fleshy triangular-shaped leaves. The daisy-like flowers are many petalled and come in yellow, pink and purple shades. The fruits are small capsules closing at the top with crossed 'fingers'. See colour section for illustration.

SEASON: The fruits appear after the flowers from late July onwards.

WHERE TO FIND: The plant originates from South Africa but has naturalised along the warm south coast of Britain and Western Europe on rocky cliffs, walls and dunes.

ROWAN OR MOUNTAIN ASH (*Sorbus aucuparia*)

The glorious thing about rowan trees is their easy accessibility; they are very popular in civic schemes for their looks and tolerant nature. Not only are the trees prettily shaped but they produce a mass of creamy white flowers that fall like confetti in late May and early June, closely followed by bunches of scarlet berries. The fruit is sharp and bitter when eaten raw, but is delicious made into a jelly; make sure you use some apples or crab apples as a base to add pectin, the vital setting agent. The preserve will be a beautiful orange colour and has a sharp, tangy flavour that is wonderful with rich meat.

DESCRIPTION: The rowan is a native deciduous tree with silvery grey bark and a rounded open crown. The pinnate leaves are divided into pairs and the flowers are borne in dense umbels. The berries are yellow when they first appear, darkening to orange and then red. See colour section for illustration.

SEASON: The berries should be fully ripe by late September, early October. Birds love them.

WHERE TO FIND: These trees are everywhere, in streets, parks, churchyards and gardens, as well as woods.

WILD STRAWBERRY (*Fragaria vesca*)

The wild strawberry is smaller and tarter than its commercial cousin and is absolutely divine. If you can gather enough fruit it makes a wonderful jam, but perhaps its scarcity is what makes the fruit so extra specially delicious. Unlike commercial strawberries the fruit freezes quite well, so you can keep gathering throughout the summer before attempting to make jam. Add the fruit to salads, or use as a finishing touch; the most glorious cake I ever tasted was a tiny cream puff studded with wild strawberries. Cook Anthony Bourdain described his first wild strawberry as '…so flavourful that it nearly took your head off'. I am reliably informed that they make an excellent liqueur when mixed with vodka and sugar, though I have not yet tried making this myself – I can never resist eating the fresh fruit (see the recipe for sloe gin on page 20 if you want to try to make your own). The botanical name comes from the Latin *fragrans*, meaning fragrant, and refers to the leaves which smell of musk when dry. Take care when drying the leaves that the process is fully completed – they should crumble when crushed. A toxin is created during drying, but when the leaf is completely dried the toxin disappears. It is possible to make tea from the leaves, which is said to help anaemia, stomach upsets and nerves, but it tastes pretty vile unless you mix it with another herb such as mint or woodruff. Wild strawberries can cause an allergic reaction in some people.

DESCRIPTION: This low-growing perennial is not a hybrid of the modern cultivated fruit, but a plant in its own right. It has deeply veined and serrated leaves and pretty, white, five-petalled flowers that appear in clusters in late spring and throughout the summer. These are followed by small red fruit. It is found throughout Europe.

SEASON: The fruit appears from summer through to early autumn; check under the plant leaves because the fruit often hides there.

WHERE TO FIND: Woodland and grassland, and chalky soils in particular.

NUTS, SEEDS AND ROOTS

Nuts and seeds are an important source of nutrition and much-neglected foodstuffs; both are high in vegetable protein and fat, dietary fibre and a range of important vitamins and minerals. Roots give vital carbohydrates, vitamins and minerals; they are the reserve food store of the plant and are packed with goodness. Seeds and nuts are generally ready for consumption when they are starting to drop naturally. Wildlife, too, is dependent on this nutritious food supply, so please be considerate when gathering.

It is illegal to dig up plant roots without first obtaining the permission of the landowner, therefore there are few that can realistically be gathered. Horseradish is probably the one exception to the rule as it often grows on wasteland and verges.

FIELD POPPY (*Papaver rhoeas*)

Ripe poppy seeds have a pleasant nutty flavour and are commonly used in the bakery, sprinkled over loaves before they go into the oven. Although poppies are commonly associated with the narcotic opium, this is derived from an entirely different species – the appropriately named *Papaver somniferum*. In fact most culinary poppy seeds originate from this species. But the seeds from the field poppy are edible too – useful if you run out when baking. The seeds should be ripe and dry – if they ping out of the seed head when it is shaken, they are ready to use. Only seeds from these species can be used for baking and all other parts of the plant are toxic.

DESCRIPTION: The poppy is believed to have originated in the Mediterranean but is now widespread across the world. The field poppy is a hardy annual that can grow to 1.2m (4ft). It carries pale grey-green leaves on a slender, hairy stem and papery red flowers succeeded by grey-green seed heads. See colour section for illustration.

SEASON: The seed heads appear from mid-summer onwards.

WHERE TO FIND: Field poppies grow on sunny roadsides, waste ground and in fields across the country.

HAZEL (*Corylus avellana*)

Hazelnuts, or cob nuts as they are otherwise known, need little introduction. Perfect specimens can be bought from the supermarket; picked from the woods they have a special flavour when fresh. Wild nuts are smaller and softer, but are a real delicacy.

DESCRIPTION: A small deciduous tree with large, heart-shaped toothed leaves. The male flowers, the catkins, are the first herald of spring, appearing in late winter. The female flowers are barely visible. The slightly flat, oval green fruit is held in a leafy surround and ripens to a warm brown. See opposite and colour section for illustration.

SEASON: Hazelnuts can be found from August onwards.

WHERE TO FIND: Hunt in woods and hedgerows: if you notice the catkins in spring you will know where to look for nuts in the autumn

100g (4oz) of hazelnuts
110g (4oz) of icing sugar

My sister Lulu makes these nuts every Christmas. First rub as much skin off the nuts as possible. Put the nuts and the icing sugar and 4–5 tablespoons of water into a heavy-based pan and bring to the boil without stirring until the water has evaporated – this takes approximately 10 minutes. Reduce the heat and continue cooking until the sugar has started to caramelise and turned a warm golden-brown colour. Put the nuts onto a sheet of lightly oiled baking parchment, separate and leave to cool. Store in an airtight container.

HORSERADISH (*Armoracia rusticana*)

Horseradish is a common plant that is easily confused with dock, until you look a little more carefully. If in doubt, crush the leaves – they give out the distinctive smell of horseradish. Plants are rather beautiful when young; the tall, oval, wavy-edged leaves look lush and inviting. The young leaves are peppery and can be a welcome addition to a salad, but the plant's principal use comes through its taproot, which has a hot, sharp, biting flavour. Made into a sauce it is a valuable accompaniment to many dishes.

The Germans and the Danes use it as an alternative to mustard and they also serve it grated raw with roast beef, as a sauce to accompany herring and mackerel, or mixed with stewed apples to make a complementary sauce for duck or goose. The root contains vitamin C, calcium, magnesium and sodium; it was thought to have antibiotic properties and was once used to treat respiratory complaints and urinary-tract infections. Be careful when peeling off the outer brown layer and when grating the root for it is very astringent; it is advisable to sit in the open air to minimise the impact of the fumes and to wear sunglasses or goggles because the sap will sting if it gets in your eye. Anyone with sensitive skin might want to wear rubber gloves too. It is a fiddly business, but worth it.

The plant seeds freely and once established it is almost impossible to kill off no matter how often you try to dig up the root. I speak from bitter experience: I indulgently allowed a clump of horseradish to establish itself in my lawn and no matter how often I try to excavate the root it always grows back. Believe me, there are limits to the amount of horseradish anyone can eat in a season!

DESCRIPTION: Horseradish is a leafy perennial native to south-eastern Europe and western Asia, and grows to about 60cm (2ft) tall. It has small white flowers that bloom from mid to late summer and a long taproot. See colour section for illustration.

SEASON: The root can be dug up and used at any time of the year. To store, cover it in sand and keep in a cool, dark place.

WHERE TO FIND: Horseradish can be found growing on grass verges and wasteland throughout Britain and Europe. The tap root goes deep into the soil and is very hard to remove completely, so don't feel too guilty about digging a root up occasionally, as you can almost guarantee that the tiniest remaining piece will manage to send up a strong new plant the following season. However, do bear in mind that it is illegal to uproot horseradish – or any other plant root – without the landowner's permission.

HORSERADISH SAUCE

Follow the advice above when handling horseradish.

3 rounded tablespoons of freshly grated horseradish
150ml (5fl oz) of soured cream
A pinch of dry mustard
Salt and pepper

Fold the grated horseradish into the soured cream; season to taste with salt, pepper and mustard. Serve with cold ham, smoked salmon or trout and hot or cold roast beef.

Sweet chestnut (*Castanea sativa*)

The Romans valued sweet chestnuts as a food crop and may well have introduced them to Britain. The fruit that you will find will be much smaller than the plump commercially grown nuts and, as anyone who has attempted it can tell you, peeling the nuts is a wearisome task. It's made somewhat, though not a great deal, easier by making a slit in the shells and then boiling them for a few minutes. The bitter skins must also be removed. Take comfort from the fact that ultra-fresh nuts are slightly easier to peel than bought ones.

When roasting nuts, make a slit in each one, reserving a single whole nut, then put them all into an open fireplace – in the hot ash is ideal. When the intact nut explodes you know that the others will be ready to eat.

Chestnut purée has innumerable uses, in casseroles, stews and stuffing. You need the patience of a saint to peel enough to make your own but the taste is worth the effort. The forest floor is thick with unused chestnuts; the profligate waste of this delicacy should spur us on to greater culinary endeavours.

DESCRIPTION: The sweet chestnut grows into the most magnificent tree with beautifully marked grey bark and long serrated leaves. The nuts are held in prickly shells and it is best to wear gloves when gathering them and extracting the nuts. See colour section for illustration.

SEASON: Chestnuts are ripe when the fruit falls to the ground, generally during October and November.

WHERE TO FIND: Sweet-chestnut trees are found in parks, gardens and woodland throughout Britain.

Sweet cicely (*Myrrhis odorata*)

Sweet cicely is a pretty plant, most commonly known as a herb; its fragrant leaves, seeds and roots impart a faint flavour of aniseed. The leaves can be chopped up and added to salads or omelettes. They are also natural sweeteners and when added to fruit while it is cooking, can reduce the amount of sugar required. The root too tastes faintly of aniseed and can be used as a vegetable – it is delicious roasted. Ripe and unripe seeds can be eaten, though ripe ones taste stronger – they are said to be a digestive aid and help to relieve flatulence when chewed!

DESCRIPTION: This plant is a hardy perennial that can grow 90cm (3ft) high. It has sturdy, hollow stems, fern-like leaves and tiny white flowers carried in clusters from late spring to early summer. See colour section for illustration.

SEASON: The seeds appear from summer onwards.

WHERE TO FIND: Sweet cicely is indigenous to Western Europe and can be found growing in woods and hedgerows.

FLOWERS

*Edible flowers are the one food that has yet to be
commercialised. You might occasionally see some
nasturtiums or courgette flowers in more select shops, but
they are something of a rarity. Flowers are principally used
for their unique and perfumed flavours, often in drinks.
Some, such as primroses and sweet violets, seem to have the
rarefied distinction of being used as cake decorations, which
does not fall fully into my definition of wild food.
Herb flowers are the exception: wild garlic flowers are
very tasty in salads and marjoram and thyme flowers
can be chopped into robust omelettes.*

Flowers are a plant's means of reproduction. Gathering
them from the wild is a breach of the Wildlife and
Countryside Act. It would be, quite literally, criminal to gather
such rarities as cowslips or primroses today for anything as
unimportant as a cake decoration or wine. Plants such as
elder or broom, however, are found everywhere and bloom
profusely, so it is unlikely that anyone would be upset by the
careful removal of a few flower heads. Whatever you pick,
always leave plenty of flowers untouched so that the plant
can reproduce and so that birds and wildlife have access to
essential fruits.

BORAGE (*Borago officinalis*)

Borage is a garden herb that rarely needs cultivating because of its propensity to self seed freely. In the ancient world it was believed to instil courage, dispel despair and induce a sense of wellbeing. Modern research has shown that it works on the adrenal gland, which affects the body's response in a crisis and may go some way to explaining its reputation. It has a high levels of calcium, potassium and mineral salts, which makes it a good general tonic and blood purifier. The young leaves have a taste pleasantly reminiscent of cucumber and are delicious chopped in a salad – the hairs seem to dissolve in the mouth. The flowers can be sprinkled onto salads or the top of summer drinks (it was a feature in the stirrup cup that ladies served to their husbands before departing to battle), frozen into ice cubes or crystallised for cake decorations.

DESCRIPTION: Borage is a pretty annual, indigenous to the Mediterranean region and now naturalised in Europe and North America, taken there by early settlers. It has stiff, prickly, hairy stems, wavy-edged silvery green leaves and beautiful blue star-like flowers and grows up to 1m (3ft).

SEASON: The plant starts to grow in April and the flowers appear from May to September.

WHERE TO FIND: Borage is commonly found on waste ground and self seeds freely.

BROOM (*Cytisus scoparius*)

Broom is a familiar cheery plant with sunny yellow flowers, found across the country on patches of open, uncultivated land. It has been used for hundreds of years and featured on the badges of kings who took their name from the plant's medieval moniker of *Planta genista*. It is also the origin of the household broom; the tough and springy stems were bound together to sweep the floor. The flower buds can be pickled in vinegar and used to replace capers in recipes. Homeopaths believe that broom is helpful in lowering blood pressure and it has been used for centuries to ease dropsy – Henry VIII is reputed to have drunk broom tea on a regular basis in his dotage.

DESCRIPTION: Broom is a deciduous shrub, although its dark green stems give the impression that it is an evergreen. Bright yellow flowers appear in late spring. See colour section for illustration.

SEASON: Flowers from April to June.

WHERE TO FIND: Heaths around Western Europe.

ELDER (*Sambucus nigra*)

The elder is a common plant with various culinary and herbal uses. There are many legends associated with it. In the past elder leaves were attached to windows and doors on the last day of April to deter witches; elder was commonly planted near the back door of the house for the same reason. It was believed that anyone standing under an elder tree at midnight on Midsummer's Eve might catch a glimpse of the King of the Elves and his retinue – though to be honest, he's proved elusive when I've put it to the test. Legend aside, the flowers have a deliciously subtle flavour commonly likened to that of muscat grapes. They can be used to make syrup, cordial, desserts and jam. The flowers can be dipped in a light batter and fried to make fritters. Elderberries are rich in vitamin C and can be used to make tasty jams and conserves. Elderberry and elderflower wines are legendary home-brewing favourites. The berries are delicious mixed in with apple crumbles and pies or added to crab apple jellies.

DESCRIPTION: The elder is a large deciduous shrub or small tree indigenous to Europe, western Asia and North Africa, and can grow to 4.5m (just under 15ft) tall. It has oval serrated leaves and flat heads of tiny creamy white flowers in late spring and early summer. These are rapidly followed by bunches of small red berries that ripen to a deep purple black. See previous page and colour section for illustration.

SEASON: The flowers appear in late April and May. The berries ripen from late August onwards and can be seen until November. When they are ripe the berry clusters hang downwards.

WHERE TO FIND: Elder enjoys a sunny position and will thrive almost anywhere; on patches of waste ground or newly cultivated soil, in hedgerows and woods.

ELDERFLOWER CORDIAL

10 large elder flowerheads, gathered when just out of bud.
900g (2lb) of sugar
2 lemons, sliced
25g (1oz) of tartaric acid

Put all the ingredients in a bowl. Add 2.3 litres (4 pints) of boiling water, cover and leave for 24 hours, stirring occasionally. Put clean bottles to warm in a low oven. Strain the cordial through muslin into the sterilised bottles. Seal and leave for a few weeks, if you can bear to wait. Dilute to taste with still or fizzy water. The cordial does not keep long, and should be used within two or three days of the bottles being opened, so it is advisable to use a number of small bottles rather than a few big ones, unless you are planning a party.

LIME (*Tilia x europaea*)

The young leaves can be used in salads or put between slices of bread and butter, but in summer the tree often becomes infested with aphids, which makes the leaves less alluring. However, it is the dried flowers that are most useful; they are used in a tea, which is not only delicious but said to be calming too – it was used as a tranquilliser by doctors during World War II. It is still a popular tea in France, where it is known as *tilleul*.

DESCRIPTION: Lime is a tall, graceful tree with a dome-shaped crown, pretty toothed, heart-shaped leaves and small, fragrant, yellowish-white flowers.

SEASON: The leaves appear in April and early May and are followed by the flowers in June and early July.

WHERE TO FIND: Common on roadsides, parks (where it is often lopped) and woodlands.

SEAWEED

Seaweed is the most remarkable plant. Not only is it packed full of goodness but it has healing properties too. Researchers investigating seaweed's nutritional qualities discovered that it is a rich source of antioxidants, such as beta carotene, and the vitamins B1 (thiamine, which keeps nerves and muscle tissue healthy), B2, riboflavin, which helps the body absorb iron, and vitamin B12.

Seaweed also contains trace elements such as chromium, which affects the way insulin behaves in the body and zinc, which helps with healing. Herbalists utilised seaweed to help them cure ailments from ulcers to cuts and grazes. Even today, dressings impregnated with seaweed are used to promote healing. The principal ingredient of thalassotherapy treatments in all the best spas is seaweed.

There is hope that seaweed might reduce the number of oestrogen-dependent diseases such as breast, ovarian and endometrial cancers. A US study found that a diet containing kelp lowers levels of the sex hormone oestradiol (a form of oestrogen). The results, published in the *American Journal of Nutrition*, may also explain why Japanese women have such a low incidence of oestrogen-dependent cancers. Seaweed comprises ten per cent of the Japanese diet. Japanese women have longer menstrual cycles and lower oestradiol levels than their western counterparts and it has long been accepted that longer menstrual cycles are linked to lower risks of female-specific cancers. In one study women with endometriosis and severe menstrual irregularities experienced significant improvement in their symptoms after taking seaweed capsules for three months.

In culinary terms seaweed is highly regarded around the world and has long been an important part of the diet of coastal communities. There are many forms that are edible, but some, such as the familiar bladder wrack with its air bladders that children so love to pop, just aren't terribly appealing – though even that can be added to stews and soups for 20 minutes to enhance flavour and act as a thickener. Here we concentrate on the best seaweeds to look for, sea vegetables you will want to use in the kitchen.

Only collect seaweed from areas where you know that the water is very clean. Use a string bag to carry it so that it can drip as you go. The plant should be thoroughly washed in fresh water before cooking.

DULSE (*Palmaria palmata*)

Dulse can be eaten raw, although it must be very finely chopped as it is quite tough. It can be added to stir fries to impart flavour and is traditionally mixed with mashed potato in parts of Ireland. In Iceland it is known as *sol* and is an important source of fibre. If you are boiling it as a vegetable make sure you start a good while before you intend to eat – it can take as long as five hours to become tender. Dulse can be added to soups and will also serve as a thickener. It has high concentrations of B12 and B6, iron, fluoride and potassium; it is also an excellent source of non-animal protein.

DESCRIPTION: The 20–50cm (8–20in) fronds are dark red to brown red with purple tints and project from a holdfast on rocks or other seaweed. The fronds are long and have rounded and sometimes divided tips.

SEASON: Best collected from May to September.

WHERE TO FIND: Dulse can be found in the lower and middle shore on rocks and stones. Take a good knife with you as the weed must be cut from its holdfast.

PURPLE LAVER (*Porphyrya umbilicalis*)

My father had fried laver bread for breakfast every morning with his bacon and egg, which was not at all unusual in Wales. It is an easy seaweed to find, particularly if you live on the English Channel or in Scotland, but it can be found all around the British coast. Try chopping it small and adding it to salads, or cook it down like spinach into a sauce or a purée – this is the basis of laver bread when mixed with oatmeal. In Scotland it is pounded into a jelly and stewed with butter to produce a jelly-like mix, which I confess I have not tried myself as it sounds fairly unappealing. It is hugely popular in Japan where it is known as *nori*. *Porphyrya palmata*, commonly known as sloke in Ireland, is much like laver, but is brown when gathered from the rocks.

DESCRIPTION: Laver is a dark red seaweed with translucent fronds of around 20cm (8in) long that look like torn wet tissue paper. It has a single stem and is attached to the rocks by a strong holdfast. It turns a green brown as it ages and black when dry.

SEASON: Best collected in spring and summer.

WHERE TO FIND: Laver clings to sand-covered rocks and boulders from mid-shore line to the lowest tidal point on exposed beaches.

Rinse the laver thoroughly and then mix it with some butter, cream, pepper and salt and heat in a pan. Add as much hot oatmeal as can be absorbed and form into small, flat rounds – or cakes. These can then be fried along with the morning bacon for breakfast.

SEA LETTUCE (*Ulva lactuca*)

Sea lettuce is a very tasty green seaweed but can be hard to find. It can be eaten raw in salads and is delicious with fish dishes and in soups; it can even be deep fried to produce a seaweed crisp. Sea lettuce is a rich source of iron and is high in vitamin C.

DESCRIPTION: recognisable by its resemblance to its namesake, sea lettuce grows in bunches of crumpled green fronds of up to 30cm (1ft) from a short stalk. New blades grow each spring.

SEASON: Best collected in spring.

WHERE TO FIND: The plant likes rocky shores and can be found along the shore in high-tide zones and on mud flats.

SEAFOOD

Shellfish used to account for 5 per cent of the total haul of the British fishing industry, but now this quota has increased to 30 per cent. British shellfish is increasingly popular and we can all, if so inclined and geographically able, collect our own from the seaside. Yet people are almost as wary about doing this as they are about collecting mushrooms. They see shellfish as potentially dangerous and only safe to eat when bought from a shop – somewhat illogical since most people will readily eat a fish they have caught without a moment's thought. The reality is that we can all safely collect our own shellfish if we care to take the trouble, but there are some common-sense rules to follow as well as some important legal restrictions.

THE PITFALLS

Oysters, mussels, razor-shells and whelks are all plentiful. However oysters and particularly mussels are best avoided unless you really know what you are doing. Both can easily be contaminated, even when living in what is technically category A seawater – ie, good and clean. A passing tanker or ferry can drop a load of sewage (even though this is illegal, it happens) and mussels and oysters can ingest this. Water contaminated with faeces contains harmful bacteria and viral pathogens which can be 100 times more concentrated in filter-feeding bivalve molluscs than in the surrounding water. It can take an oyster one week to cleanse itself after contamination, but it can take a mussel three months, which is why they are best avoided altogether.

Basically there is no way that you can tell by looking at a shellfish whether or not it is safe to eat. The oysters and mussels you buy will have been through purification tanks for several days and these are regularly checked to ensure that if a polluted shellfish goes in, it will, theoretically, be clear by the time it comes out. A friendly local oyster farmer told me that he would never eat a fresh oyster or mussel that had not been through purification tanks, though he did allow that if he was somewhere where the water was spectacularly clear he might just consider it. Crabs and lobsters are safer because they catch their own food and do not filter it via the water.

IN PRAISE OF OYSTERS

Cook Anthony Bourdain describes his first oyster as a seminal experience in his book *A Cook's Tour*: 'I've never forgotten that moment: that big, scary, ugly shell in my neighbour's knobbly hand, the way he popped it open for me, still dripping from the bay, the way its pale, blue-grey flesh caught the light, pulsated, the mother-of-pearl-like interior of the shell like a jewel box – promising adventure, freedom, sex, as-yet-unencountered joys.' It makes my first taste of an oyster feel a bit lame by comparison (I wasn't very impressed!) but I am now a keen connoisseur.

Shellfish cannot be eaten by the faint hearted. The first rule of safety is that you can only eat an animal that was alive before cooking: anything that is already dead must be discarded. Crabs and lobsters should be alive and kicking and cockles must open up on cooking. All shellfish can be eaten at any time of the year – even oysters, despite the old rule that they shouldn't be eaten when there is an 'r' in the month. The sound reasoning for this is that these are the months when the oysters are spawning and whether you are farming oysters or foraging for them, you do not want your supply to dry up. Whatever the time of year you collect them, eat your shellfish straight away – the fresher the better; they don't have a long shelf life.

FOLLOWING THE LAW

It is not only lacking in common sense to hunt small sea creatures, it can also be a criminal offence. There are minimum sizes of crabs, lobsters, whelks and so on, that you are allowed to collect, and a limit to the number you can gather for personal use. This varies from area to area and is governed by local Sea Fisheries Committees – contact numbers can be obtained via DEFRA, the Department for Environment, Food and Rural Affairs (see Useful Organisations, page 92). The National Trust, for example, would not want specimens taken from its land without authorisation. The best way to be sure that you are not breaking any rules is to speak to the local harbour master. Some areas are out of bounds altogether and only people with shellfish permits are allowed to fish or forage. Large notices usually proclaim this fact, but it is always wise to speak to the local authorities before having a go yourself – often they will direct you to the most fruitful areas. Some shellfish have become scarce through overfishing and for that reason I would not encourage you to hunt for scallops, a prime example.

The whelk is really just a sea snail, and if you like snails you'll probably adore whelks – they are one of those foods you either love or hate. Whelks must have a minimum landing size shell length of 45mm (1¾in). They need to be cooked for about 20 minutes; you have to use a pin, and twist, to extract them from their shell. If they don't come away they are not properly cooked and should be discarded. If overcooked they turn to jelly very quickly.

GETTING THE CHILDREN INVOLVED

All children should learn how to find or catch cockles, whelks, crabs and lobsters. In Noel Streatfeild's blissful children's book *The Growing Summer*, a family of city children are sent to live with their great aunt Dymphna and are left at a loss as to what they should do. Aunt Dymphna replies: 'You have the whole wing of the house to yourselves. This magnificent kitchen. The glorious world outside to play in. All that the earth brings forth to feed you and you stand there asking stupid questions until my head reels. Help yourselves, children, help yourselves.' Needless to say, by the end of the summer the children are catching mackerel, prawns and lobster and much the better and all the nicer for it.

COCKLE (*Cerastoderma edule*)

The pretty cockle shell is immediately recognisable by toddlers upwards thanks to illustrations to the nursery rhyme Mary Mary Quite Contrary. Cockles are plentiful and can be found in densities of 10,000 per square metre. Don't eat cockles that aren't buried or which have green on them – this is a sign of an unhealthy creature. When you have a haul of cockles rinse them quickly to remove excess sand and grit, then place them in a bucket of clean salted water, with some flour added. The cockles will eat the flour, get a little fatter and at the same time discharge grit. To cook, place the cockles in boiling water, return the pan to the boil and simmer for just four minutes. If the meat is still attached to the shell after this time it is best discarded. To separate the cooked meat from the shells, drop them into boiling water with a high salt density: the meat will float to the top and can be lifted out with a slatted spoon, the shells will sink.

DESCRIPTION: The shell comes in a variety of creamy brown tones. It is finely ribbed and has concentric circles across its ribs. See below for illustration.

SEASON: Cockles can be found throughout the year.

WHERE TO FIND: Cockles like sand and fine gravel so look for likely areas at low tide and take a rake, shovel, sieve and bucket with you – though, believe me, a child's bucket and spade will suffice. Dig around and you will find the cockles easily enough, but only take the bigger ones.

GRAHAM'S COCKLE RECIPE

Leave cockles for 24 hours to purify in salt water, as detailed on page 49. Cook for four minutes in salted water and separate from their shells. Put some olive oil into a pan, gently fry a finely chopped onion with a few cloves of garlic. Add the

cockles along with a couple of glasses of white wine, some cream and a handful of finely chopped parsley and serve hot.

EDIBLE CRAB (*Cancer pagurus*)

The serious heavyweight specimens are found at sea, but younger crabs are plentiful and easy to find if you look under stones. Please don't take small crabs – there are restrictions as to the precise size you are allowed to take away and this varies according to the location. EU regulations state that crabs must be a minimum of 140mm (5½in) carapace (main shell) length, but in Cornwall the UK size for male edible crabs is set at 160mm (6¼in). It is important to establish what size of crab you can harvest locally. Similarly you need to determine the numbers that you are allowed to take: once again the amounts can vary from area to area, from a limit of five lobsters and 25 crabs to one or two lobsters and ten crabs.

DESCRIPTION: Edible crabs have a flat and smooth red-brown shell, the edge of which is crimped like a pie crust. The claws have black tips. See below for illustration.

SEASON: Crabs, like lobsters, can be found throughout the year, but hunting in winter is miserable, so stick to the warmer months.

WHERE TO FIND: Put on a pair of boots, head out at low tide and turn over rocks – the crabs will be beneath them.

LOBSTER (*Homarus gammarus*)

Lobster is generally regarded as one of the great seafood delicacies, not least because it is so expensive – often prohibitively so. However, lobsters are easier to find than you might think: a friend from Kent reported that while out looking for worms for fishing in Herne Bay at an exceptionally low tide, he found 25 lobsters! Needless to say he put all but one back, which is what foraging is all about.

Cooking a lobster is probably the closest many of us get to the harsh reality of real-life hunting. The lobster is live and must be killed if you are to eat it. Research has found that the most compassionate way to dispatch a lobster is to place it into the freezer for several hours, which renders it insensate, then drop it into boiling water. The minimum size lobster you can collect should have a carapace length of 87mm (3½in), excluding tail and pincers.

DESCRIPTION: Lobsters have brown-black shells and the front walking legs carry a pair of massive pincers. Size varies enormously: the largest specimens, which can reach up to 1m (3ft), are probably around 50 years old. Lobsters most commonly caught in lobster pots are around 15cm (6in) long and are approximately four to five years old.

SEASON: Lobsters can be caught throughout the year; however, hunting for them in winter is pure misery.

WHERE TO FIND: Lobsters live in holes and excavated tunnels from the lower shore to sea depths of 60m (65½yd) – the bigger lobsters live further out to sea. Take a metal stick with a curled end and when you see an indentation under a rock push the stick into the sand and then pull towards you.

RAZOR-SHELL (*Ensis siliqua* and *Ensis arcuatus*)

Razor-shells are hugely underrated; I prefer them to mussels, though they are quite different in texture. They have a delicate flavour and I cannot recommend them highly enough. They are plentiful: you see their shells littering many British beaches – if the shells are there, you can guarantee that the live clam will be there too. They are quick and easy to cook and look very pretty on the plate when served. Don't take away the longest razors: if they are bigger than 13cm (5in) they tend to be tougher, but also, purely on the practical side, they are harder to fit in the pan and on the plate. However, you must not remove clams under 10cm (4in) according to EU legislation. Try the recipe on the following page, or use them in paella.

DESCRIPTION: Razors live in burrows in the sand; they dig rapidly using a strong, muscular foot and can be out of sight in seconds. At high tide they come closer to the surface of the sand and push out a siphon for feeding and breathing.

SEASON: Do not collect razor clams in winter and spring as this is their time to spawn.

WHERE TO FIND: Walk along the shore at low tide. Razors live in sand, so when you see an indentation and a hole in the sand pour a little salt into the hole and wait – after just a few minutes the razor will come up to the surface and can be pulled out.

This recipe comes courtesy of Warren Beesley, head chef of the gastro pub The Pearson's Arms on the seafront in Whitstable. To say it is delicious is an understatement. The recipe is for one person, so multiply as required.

7 razor-shells
1 dessertspoon of butter
¼ of a lemon
Salt and pepper
Chopped parsley

Clean the razor-shells by washing them – ideally with salt water, but fresh will do, and leave to drain. Warm a pan, put in the razor-shells, add the butter, the juice of the lemon and one rub or downward stroke on the grater of zest from the lemon. Add salt and pepper and some chopped parsley, cover the pan and cook for approximately one minute – if razor-shells are cooked any longer they tend to get tough. Put the razor-shells on a plate in their shells, pour over the lemon butter mixture and serve with a few slices of good fresh bread.

FUNGI

There is more nervousness about collecting fungi than virtually any other form of wild food. The fact is that there are a lot of myths attached to what is and what isn't safe to eat and in the case of wild fungi it is as though we are infected with an irrational and all-encompassing fear. I blame all those lurid fairy tales from childhood: virtually every fantastic illustration hints at danger with a liberal sprinkling of red-and-white spotted toadstools – these outsize growths also serve as a home to all manner of nasty sprites. No wonder we instinctively back away in fear when we come across them in a wood. Yet wild mushrooms, of all forms of wild food, can offer some of the most perfect taste experiences and are lauded by such culinary luminaries as Jane Grigson and Antonio Carluccio.

One cultivated mushroom dominates the commercial market – *Agaricus bisporus*. It comes as button, closed-cup and open-cup options, all of which are exactly the same species: the shape changes as the mushroom matures – button mushrooms are the youngest. More recently the range has extended and even in supermarkets exotic varieties such as dried shiitake, oyster and porcini are readily available.

IDENTIFICATION

Wild fungi, which cannot be re-created in any commercial environment, are often blessed with the most exquisite or distinctive flavours. If you want to enjoy them then you have to learn how to identify them. There are many more edible wild varieties than there are poisonous ones. Some of the edible varieties, while safe to eat, won't have anything particular in the flavour department to recommend them. However, I am not recommending that you give fungi collecting a go on the basis that you are more likely to pick a safe one than a poisonous one.

Some fungi can make you very ill indeed. Some can kill you. Some varieties can be eaten and regarded as a great delicacy by some people, but the same variety of mushroom will give other people a stomach upset. Finally, some mushrooms are edible – but only when they have been cooked to destroy the toxins within – the cooking process renders them safe. When eating any mushroom for the first time always cook it first and eat only a small piece in case of adverse reaction.

It is very important that you learn how to recognise the different varieties and remember even these can vary in appearance from the textbook description due to age or the environment. No amount of reading, however good the book, can replace practical field experience with an expert on hand to guide you. It won't take long for you to be confident about recognising the most delicious edible mushrooms and this is a skill that can then be passed down from generation to generation. There are field courses available around the country; many are supported by local authorities. Alternatively, you can go to the British Mycological Society, the Association of British Fungus Groups, or the Wildlife Trusts for advice on where to find a course locally (see Useful Organisations, page 92).

No specialist equipment is required to gather mushrooms, but you are advised to take a knife for cutting and a brush to remove excess leaf matter or soil on site. Never pull fungi out of the ground: cutting the stem rather than pulling it will help the fungi regenerate and keep the supply going.

EUROPEAN ATTITUDES

In Europe they are far less squeamish about collecting fungi from the wild. In Italy there are experts who visit towns and villages on a regular basis and who can be consulted on what is safe to eat and what is not. In France many chemists offer a similar service and dogs are trained to sniff out truffles. Elizabeth David details the delight of hunting the elusive white truffle in the Italian town of Alba in her book *An Omelette and a Glass of Wine*: '…there are baskets of prime mushrooms to look at and to smell, chestnut and ochre coloured *funghi porcini*, the cèpes or *Boletus edulis* common in the wooded countryside of Piedmont, and some fine specimens of the beautiful red-headed *Amanita caesara*, the young of which are enclosed in an egg-shaped white cocoon, or volva, which has earned them the name of *funghi uovali*, egg mushrooms. They are the *oronges* considered by some French fungi-fanciers as well as by the Piedmontese to be the best of all mushrooms.'

FOLLOW THE CODE OF CONDUCT

There is a code of conduct for wild mushroom pickers to follow. Some of its advice is standard – no one should damage the environment in which they work, nor should they collect species that are rare, nor collect mushrooms they do not intend to eat. Mushroom pickers are asked to never pick more than 1.5kg (3lb) of mushrooms at a time, or no more than half of the fruiting bodies of any single species present, whichever is the lower amount. Button mushrooms should not be collected – only take mushrooms that have opened – this way not only do you get bigger mushrooms, but you also allow the spores to be discharged.

Always seek permission from the landowner to hunt for fungi. You should also be aware that you will not be able to collect fungi from SSSIs (Sites of Special Scientific Interest) or on most nature reserves. The fines for collecting on either can be quite significant. Don't pick mushrooms from busy roadsides where they will have been exposed to pollution, or from fields that may have been sprayed with pesticides.

AGE MATTERS

The mushroom is the fruiting body of the fungus and it provides a protective cover for the gills, which bear the spores. The earliest stage of the mushroom – the button – does not reveal enough of the characteristics of the mushroom for safe identification, so do not collect immature mushrooms that cannot be positively identified. By the same token old mushrooms can become infested with insects and decay rapidly and are best left alone. The shape, texture, colour and perfume of the mushroom, along with the appearance of its gills (some fungi have tubes and pores instead of gills), roots and spore colour are significant aides to identification.

Taking a spore print from a mushroom is easy; remove the stem from the mushroom and place it on a piece of paper (half black paper and half white is advisable as spore colours range from chocolate to white or pink), cover it with a jar and leave for a few hours.

Mushrooms are only available for short seasons, so if you want to extend their availability you will need to dry them. Collect on a dry day, clean and dry them as necessary, then slice them and lay slices on a piece of paper. Leave somewhere warm for a few days. When the mushrooms are completely dry they can be stored in airtight jars as they are, or put into a liquidiser until you have finely chopped mushrooms for flavouring casseroles and soups. Before you use the mushrooms place them in a bowl of hot water for at least half an hour.

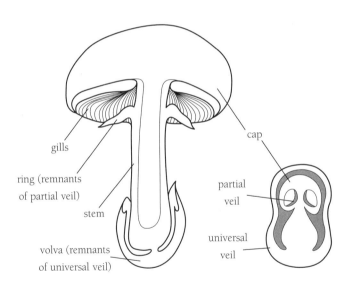

gills

cap

ring (remnants of partial veil)

partial veil

stem

universal veil

volva (remnants of universal veil)

Mature fruit body   Developing fruit body

CEP (*Boletus edulis*)

The cep is a delicious mushroom suitable for gourmet palettes; it is very much appreciated in Europe where it is better known by its Italian name, *porcini*. Before cooking, the pores of the cep should be removed; use a spoon, so that you are just left with the flesh of the cap. It is delicious eaten raw in salads, but equally will enhance any number of dishes. Eaten fresh, ceps are at their best when young, but they also dry very well and are useful to have on standby. When you pick a cep, break off a small piece of the cap: if the flesh stays white it is a cep, but if it changes colour you will have gathered another similar species. Some of these are inedible and one is poisonous – this has distinctive red stripes at its base and when the fungi is mature the pores turn a similar colour, so it is hard to confuse with a true cep.

DESCRIPTION: The cep has a smooth, dry, polished top, that looks somewhat like a bun and which measures 5–30cm (2–12in) in diameter. The underside is a mass of yellowish, sponge-like pores and the stem is short, swollen and coloured fawn and white. The cap looks increasingly polished as the fungi ages. See colour section for illustration.

SEASON: August to November.

WHERE TO FIND: Ceps appear in woodland clearings.

CHANTERELLE (*Cantharellus cibarius*)

The chanterelle is a beautiful mushroom with distinctive egg-yolk yellow flesh; on menus it often goes by its French name *girolle*, and is wonderful cooked with omelettes or scrambled eggs. It can be bitter when raw and so should be cooked before eating, even if it is only used in salads – it is delicious fried. The chanterelle is so distinctive that it is hard to confuse, making it a good starting point for would-be collectors. The false chanterelle looks somewhat similar, but like the perma-tanned footballer's wife it is more orange in colour – and it lacks the distinctive smell of apricot.

DESCRIPTION: The chanterelle ranges in diameter from 2–15cm (¾–6in). It has blunt ridges instead of gills, which flare upwards and outwards to the lip of the horn so that the centre of the cap is depressed. It has a distinctive scent like that of ripe plums or apricots. See colour section for illustration.

SEASON: June to October.

WHERE TO FIND: Chanterelles thrive in mixed and coniferous woods; they are often found close to beech trees, birch trees or on mossy banks.

FIELD BLEWIT (*Lepista saeva*)

The blewit has distinctive violet to blue stems, hence its common name of blue legs. It was very popular in the Midlands and was traditionally regarded as an acceptable substitute for tripe. It is generally used as flavouring for soups and stews. The wood blewit (*Lepista nuda*) is smaller and more delicate but the colour of its cap, gills and stalk are a more pronounced violet blue. It has a more subtle flavour, but should not be eaten raw. It can be found in deciduous and coniferous woods. When eating either mushroom for the first time only have a small piece as they can cause stomach upsets in some people.

DESCRIPTION: The pale brown to grey caps are flat and irregular and curl under at the edges; they have a diameter of 5–13cm (2–5in). The flesh has a translucent, jelly-like appearance. The gills are white or greyish pink and the blue to violet stems are swollen at the base. See colour section for illustration.

SEASON: Blewits appear from October and can continue to appear into the New Year.

WHERE TO FIND: These fungi grow in rough pastures, often in rings, and are best picked in dry weather.

GIANT PUFFBALL (*Lycoperdon giganteum*)

This is one of the more astonishing fungi – a mighty
mushroom, virtually the size of a football, will suddenly
appear in a field or on the edge of a wood. Just one of these
can serve a number of people since every bit is edible. The
only important thing to check is that the flesh is white when
you cut into it; if the flesh is yellowing or grey it has moved
past its best-by date. It is very good cut into steaks and fried
with a little garlic and olive oil and extra delicious if dipped
first in beaten egg and then breadcrumbs. Antonio Carluccio
recommends it fried in olive oil with some garlic, chopped
parsley and thyme and lemon juice. The giant puffball can't
be preserved for future use, so enjoy it fresh.

DESCRIPTION: This mighty white sphere can measure
anything from 10–30cm (4–12in). See colour section
for illustration.

SEASON: Between July and November.

WHERE TO FIND: The giant puffball grows in meadows,
gardens, under hedges and on the edges of woodland.

MOREL (*Morchella esculenta*)

This is a very popular wild mushroom for culinary use. It has a wonderful flavour cooked solo but seems to work beautifully in any number of other dishes, including omelettes, risottos, soups and stews. Morels should only be picked when they are firm and young. They must be washed thoroughly, but in addition it is advisable to boil them in water for a few minutes to get rid of dead insects or grit. They should not be eaten raw. Take care not to confuse these fungi with false morel. The stem of the false morel is multi chambered, like its cap, whereas the stem of the true morel is not. Morels both freeze and dry successfully; cut them in half before drying.

DESCRIPTION: The morel doesn't look like a typical mushroom; it has a cap that looks like a sponge or honeycomb pitted with deep depressions, and a short, stout stem. The cap is conical and has a diameter of 8–15cm (3–6in). The colour can vary from pale yellow to nearly black. See colour section for illustration.

SEASON: The fungi appear in spring but only for a few days.

WHERE TO FIND: Morels can be found near trees and hedgerows; they often grow on ground that has been burnt.

St George's mushroom (*Calocybe gambosa*)

The beauty of this mushroom is that it tends to appear first around St George's Day, 23rd April – hence its name – which is tremendously helpful in the first stage of identification. It tastes best when young, and is much sought after by the French who appreciate its distinctive taste. It can be dried.

DESCRIPTION: St George's mushroom has a flattish cap with a wavy margin. It can be white or buff in colour and has a diameter of 5–15cm (2–6in). The stem and gills are both white. See colour section for illustration. It can be confused with red-staining inocybe, which is poisonous, but which has reddish fibres on the cap and pink to brown gills.

SEASON: Between April and June.

WHERE TO FIND: In woods, hedgerows, pastures and roadsides. The St George's mushroom likes chalky soil; it can form large rings, so if you find one more may well be close by.

PLANT LEAVES

Greens make up a hugely important part of our diet. Not only do they have the fringe benefit of being very low in calories, but they are high in phytochemicals such as vitamins C and A, lutein and folic acid. They contain plenty of dietary fibre and are high in iron and calcium.

All our favourite green vegetables and salads have their origins in the wild and have been cultivated over the centuries to produce the taste we know today. The most common complaint about commercially grown fruit and vegetables today is that flavour has been compromised in favour of uniformity and outsize growth. The backlash has begun and small growers are returning to older varieties to produce tastier products. Some professional foragers are marketing their wares on the internet and offer all sorts of wild and wonderful goods, though this does seem to rather undermine the whole point of gathering from the wild – you should make time to do it yourself.

GREENS ARE GOOD FOR THE BODY AND MIND

The time pressures on our society make gathering wild food therapeutic, even addictive. Foraging gets you out in the fresh air, brings you closer to your local environment and forces you to take a complete break from day-to-day stresses. It becomes a pure pleasure.

The flavour of wild greens will stimulate the palate. Young leaves, shoots and stems have the most delicate flavour and are often the tastiest: this is because the essential oils in the plant leaves become more concentrated with age – most commercially grown vegetables are picked when immature. Hawthorn leaf buds and leaves are a prime example: delicious when young, but rapidly becoming just another tough old green with no flavour to recommend them. Fortuitously, other greens have a longer season; sea beet can be picked from March to November as long as you don't strip plants bare, giving them a chance to recover.

Once you start eating wild greens you will find that you are constantly plucking leaves off this and that to sample, and crave all sorts of new taste experiences. The village of Tide Head in New Brunswick, Canada claims to be the fiddlehead capital of the world. I long to try the young unfolding shoots of the fiddlehead fern, which, at an early point in their growth, resemble the head of a fiddle. However, they have to be very carefully cooked and their water must be changed regularly during the process to remove toxins and tannins; very time consuming, but far more exciting than buying broccoli from the supermarket.

ALEXANDERS (*Smyrnium olusatrum*)

Alexanders or black lovage has been an important pot herb for centuries. The stems and leaves have a flavour akin to a blend of celery and parsley. It can be used raw in salads when young and tender, or in soups and casseroles later in the season. The seeds have a peppery flavour and, theoretically, can be substituted for pepper. The botanical name is derived from the Greek for myrrh and alludes to the plant's sweet, perfumed flavour.

DESCRIPTION: This is a tall, hardy biennial that can reach 1.5m (5ft) high. It has large, glossy, serrated leaves and tall flower stems topped with white umbels, which in turn produce black seeds. See colour section for illustration. Lovage (*Levisticum officinale*) has similar uses and looks, though it has yellow flowers and is not as commonly found in the UK.

SEASON: Alexanders appear in March and flowers in May. The black seeds – a useful indicator for the novice – are visible by late June and July.

WHERE TO FIND: The plant is commonly found on the roadside and on wasteland, especially around the coast.

CHICKWEED (*Stellaria media*)

Chickweed was once commonly sold on city streets both as a green vegetable and a cure for a wide range of ailments – chickweed infusions were used to aid weight loss. It is a classic example of a plant that gardeners regard as a weed; for if left unchecked it romps all over the flower borders. It is in fact a great bonus, for you can harvest it for free and weed at the same time. It is a delicious substitute for cress: chickweed sandwiches are a great favourite with my children. Use the whole plant in salads or cook gently as a vegetable; it only requires a minute or two on a gentle heat in some butter to be ready. Birds love the seed – hence the name.

DESCRIPTION: Chickweed is a fine-rooted annual with soft, pale green, oval leaves that run in pairs along the prostrate stems, which can vary in length from 5–40cm (2–16in) and have a single line of hairs along their length. It has small, white, star-like flowers up to 1cm (½in) across. See right and colour section for illustration.

SEASON: Chickweed can be seen year round in mild conditions.

WHERE TO FIND: It likes bare and cultivated ground and will often appear on a new seed bed.

DANDELION (*Taraxacum officinale*)

The dandelion is a common weed with the apparent advantage of being readily available. The plants used to be so popular that they were carefully cultivated in the kitchen gardens of the finest homes. It is still very popular in France as a salad leaf, where it is served with chives, parsley and garlic and dressed with oil and lemon juice. Gathering the leaves is in theory easy enough, but don't pick them from your lawn if you have pets. The real secret to success with this plant is not to eat any old leaf, but to allow some to grow in the herbaceous border, feed them and put a cardboard tube or flower pot over the foliage to produce a bigger and more delicate-tasting leaf. The root can be eaten – try roasting it in oil.

DESCRIPTION: Deep-toothed, glossy, green leaves grow in rosettes from the base of the plant. Tall yellow flowers appear on fleshy stems with a milky sap from March to November.

SEASON: Fairly young leaves should be picked before the plant comes into flower.

WHERE TO FIND: Dandelions can be found on grass verges, pastures and lawns throughout Britain and Europe.

FAT HEN (*Chenopodium album*)

Fat hen is a common wild plant that quickly takes over new patches of land or waste ground when the opportunity presents itself. It has been eaten since Neolithic times; its ready availability meant that it was a staple green for centuries. Its Saxon name, *melde*, is reflected in East Anglian village names, such as Meldreth, and signifies how important the plant was as a food source. The leaves, like its close relative spinach, are a good source of vitamin B1 and are rich in iron, protein and calcium, and although less convenient than its commercial cousin, it is actually even more nutritious. Cook young leaves and shoots as you would spinach – very quickly in water or butter.

DESCRIPTION: This tall annual plant has reddish stems that readily reach 1m (3ft) tall. It has oval-toothed green leaves and spiked clusters of small white flowers and is covered in a fine powdery meal. The tiny seeds are dark brown. See colour section for illustration.

SEASON: Leaves first appear in March and continue through to October.

WHERE TO FIND: This plant, like stinging nettles, prefers nitrogen-rich soil, as in compost heaps. It can be found on both cultivated ground and wasteland all over Britain.

FENNEL (*Foeniculum vulgare*)

Fennel is a glorious plant. Not only does it look beautiful, but all parts of it are edible. It has been consumed for centuries: the Romans and the Greeks used it as a slimming aid and Anglo Saxons ate it on fasting days to help stave off hunger pangs. The fennel bulb we buy in the supermarket comes from Florence fennel, but you can also eat the much smaller bulb of wild fennel. The leaves, which have a delicate aniseed flavour, are best eaten when young and fresh; but as they can appear as early as December and January in mild winters and go on producing leaf until June, they have a long season. The leaves are delicious chopped over new potatoes or sprinkled over fish. Fennel tea is supposed to be helpful to babies with colic – getting them to drink the tea is quite another matter. The best solution is for a breast-feeding mother to drink the infusion instead. To make the tea put a teaspoon of seeds into a cup and add boiling water. Strain the liquid and discard the seeds before drinking.

DESCRIPTION: Fennel is a striking hardy perennial, indigenous to Asia and the Mediterranean regions. It reaches a statuesque 1.5m (5ft) tall and is cloaked with a froth of bright green feathery foliage and topped by yellow flowers in large umbels. See colour section for illustration.

SEASON: Fennel first appears in early spring or late winter and flowers from June onwards. The seeds are ripe and ready for harvesting by late October.

WHERE TO FIND: Fennel is common in coastal regions where it can be seen on roadsides, cliff tops and on wasteland.

GOOD KING HENRY
(*Chenopodium bonus-henricus*)

Good King Henry has distinctly tangy and sharp-flavoured leaves which, like sorrel and rhubarb, contain oxalic acid and should be eaten in moderation by anyone suffering from rheumatism, arthritis, gout or bladder stones. The leaves and shoots are delicious when young and are also rich in iron, but become bitter when old. However, the young leaves can be picked off continuously throughout the growing season. You can even try cooking the young flower buds. There is some debate as to the source of its common name, whether it refers to Henry IV of France or a Saxon elf – either way it serves as a reminder of its longevity as a valued food source.

DESCRIPTION: This perennial herb can grow 30–60cm (1–2ft) tall. It has broad triangular leaves with wavy edges and a powdery surface. The insignificant flower spikes appear from May to August. See right for illustration.

SEASON: The first leaves appear in April and can be picked until August.

WHERE TO FIND: Look on roadsides, waste ground and on cultivated ground.

Ground elder (*Aegopodium podagraria*)

Gardeners curse ground elder for its propensity to take over the herbaceous borders, but I have a sneaking fondness for it for it is actually a very pretty plant, with beautiful frothing white flower heads. The fact that it is good to eat is all the better. It may not be a crop whose location you can altogether control, but if you develop a flexible approach you will have a ready supply of a tasty vegetable on tap. The leaves are aromatic and have a tangy flavour and should be cooked like spinach; they can be eaten raw in salads if you appreciate the taste or added to soups for flavour. The plant is also known as herb Gerrard: the story runs that St Gerrard administered the plant to monks who had prayed that they might be relieved of gout. An infusion of the leaves reportedly brought them speedy relief, after which the plant became established in medieval herb gardens.

DESCRIPTION: This invasive perennial has three-lobed, oval-toothed leaves that appear from May to July. The white flowers are produced in June and are arranged in umbels on tall stems of up to around 1m (3ft). See colour section for illustration.

SEASON: Shoots appear in April or even earlier in a mild winter.

WHERE TO FIND: The plant likes shade and is common in gardens, on roadsides and on waste ground in Britain and Europe.

HAWTHORN (*Crataegus monogyna*)

Hawthorn or May is one of more common native British trees and while ornamental varieties have been planted in parks and gardens, the original is found in woods and hedges throughout the land. The young leaf buds have a pleasant taste and can be served in sandwiches as a spring green. Richard Mabey, wild-food guru, recommends chopping them up to add to a new potato salad. The berries are perfectly safe to eat, but are nothing special raw; use them to make an unusual fruit jelly to accompany meat.

DESCRIPTION: This prickly deciduous tree has cracked pink-brown bark and small three- or seven-lobed leaves. It is smothered in tiny white or pink five-petalled flowers in April and May, followed by red berries. See below and colour section for illustration.

SEASON: Leaves can be picked in April and May; berries should be used within two weeks of ripening.

WHERE TO FIND: Woodland, hedgerows and parkland.

HOP (*Humulus lupulus*)

The hop is an attractive climbing plant with pale lime flowers. The Romans ate it as a vegetable and by the 8th century its flavouring and preserving qualities had been discovered and were widely used in the brewing industry to impart a bitter flavour. The shoots are considered a great delicacy in Belgium, Germany and France. Cook them like asparagus in boiling salted water and serve with eggs or in a risotto. Try making an omelette with hop shoots. First cook the hop shoots briefly in butter; then in a separate pan make your omelette and when it is beginning to set, add the shoots, some cream cheese and some chopped tarragon and chives. Flip the omelette in half and serve. Hop leaves can be added to soup, but should be blanched in boiling water first to remove the bitterness. Elizabeth David recommends that you cook the shoots in olive oil, with garlic and ham, before covering with water and continuing to cook gently to make a soup, which can be further enriched with the addition of eggs, one for each person being served. The hop is both a sedative and a soporific – hence the popularity of hop pillows. An infusion of flowers makes a mild sedative, but the flowers can be added to other herbal teas as a digestive aid and appetite stimulant.

DESCRIPTION: Hops are strongly growing hardy perennials with twining stems. The new shoots, which twist in a clockwise direction, grow to heights of 7.5m (25ft) before dying back in the autumn. The large, attractive leaves have three to five lobes. Male and female flowers are borne on separate plants: male flowers are tiny and are borne in clusters; the female flowers are the more familiar cone-like formation of papery, overlapping bracts and are the source of the hop's essential oils. See colour section for illustration.

SEASON: Pick the young side shoots in spring and the flowers in early autumn.

SEASON: Pick the young side shoots in spring and the flowers in early autumn.

WHERE TO FIND: Hops like rich soils and are often found in hedgerows and on the outskirts of woods.

LEMON BALM (*Melissa officinalis*)

Lemon balm has been used as a culinary and medicinal herb for centuries. The flavour of the leaves is quite delicate; it can be used to replace lemon rind or lemon grass in recipes. It is reputed to ease headaches and tension and to restore the memory. A cup of tea made with a few mint and lemon balm leaves is said to aid digestion and a cup of lemon balm tea at bedtime to induce sleep. Drinking leaves and flowering tips may help promote longevity. In the 13th century Prince Llewellyn of Glamorgan claimed he drank Melissa tea daily and according to legend he lived to a ripe old age of 108. Pop a few leaves into a cup of boiling water, leave for five minutes, strain and discard leaves before drinking.

DESCRIPTION: Lemon balm is a half-hardy perennial indigenous to southern and central Europe. The plant has aromatic veined and toothed light green leaves and insignificant yellow flowers throughout the summer and into autumn.

SEASON: The new stems appear in March and are at their best in April and May when flowering begins. The flavour and scent of leaves that have been in full sun can become rather harsh.

WHERE TO FIND: The Romans introduced the herb to Britain and it became a regular in apothecaries' gardens. It is very invasive and has become naturalised in wasteland in southern England.

SEA BEET (*Beta vulgaris maritima*)

Sea beet is one of my favourite vegetables; it grew close to my last house on a patch of wasteland and had the attraction of being easy to gather, with the additional benefit of a long growing season. Once a week men would come with sacks to gather the leaves to sell to some of the best London restaurants; the leaves are small so you have to be patient when picking. The leaf tastes like a superior spinach, and does not collapse into pulp quite as quickly on cooking, but retains its texture. The youngest leaves, which are preferable, can also be eaten raw in salads; they are also tasty in quiche and soup.

DESCRIPTION: The plant can be annual, biennial or perennial. It has shiny, pointed oval leaves and insignificant green clusters of flowers that are borne on spikes from May to August. See colour section for illustration.

SEASON: Leaves can be picked from March to November.

WHERE TO FIND: This plant is, as its name suggests, common around the coastland of Britain and southern and western Europe.

SORREL (*Rumex acetosa*)

Sorrel has a distinctive lemony or fruity tang to its leaves and is a truly delicious addition to early salads; it can also be used as a pot herb later in the year. The plant has diuretic and cooling properties, is high in vitamins A, B and C and is rich in potassium. Romans used to eat the leaves to settle their stomachs after overeating and Roman soldiers used to suck the leaves to take the edge off their thirst. This habit gave the plant its name, which comes from the Latin *rumo* meaning 'I suck'. It can be used in omelettes as a flavouring, or as an accompaniment to fish. The leaves cook terribly quickly; you really only need to introduce them to a little butter or water. Sorrel, like rhubarb, is high in oxalic acid and should be used in moderation by anyone suffering from rheumatism, arthritis, gout or bladder stones. Use stainless steel utensils for cutting and cooking, as contact with iron spoils the flavour of the leaves. My daughter, who had a natural aversion to any and all greens when small, would consume this leaf with great relish!

DESCRIPTION: Sorrel has distinctive arrow-shaped leaves and small red and green flower stalks that appear from May to August. See colour section for illustration.

SEASON: This is one of the earliest greens to appear; the leaves are tastiest when young and fresh in March.

WHERE TO FIND: The plant can be found throughout Europe on wasteland, roadsides and in meadows.

STINGING NETTLE (*Urtica dioica*)

The infamous stinging nettle ranks as the most common wild herb in temperate regions throughout the world. It is packed with goodness, being rich in vitamins A and C as well as containing iron and other minerals. It has been an important food source in times of shortage, notably during the great potato famine and during World War II. Nettle soup is delicious, absolutely zinging with goodness and is very easy to make. Just remember to take scissors, rubber gloves and a plastic bag with you for protection when gathering the leaves. The cooking process destroys the formic acid in the leaves and renders the plant safe to eat. Nettle tea is reputed to help cleanse the system and may alleviate hay fever and some skin allergies. To make it chop a few nettle leaves (wearing gloves), put them in a jug and cover with boiled water. Leave for five minutes before straining and serving. Drink three times a day.

DESCRIPTION: The stinging nettle grows up to 1.2m (4ft) high. The toothed and veined oval leaves are covered with fine hairs or hollow needles that break easily on contact, releasing formic acid, which irritates the skin. Insignificant green flowers appear from summer through to autumn.

SEASON: Young leaves first appear in February and can be used in the kitchen until flowering commences in early June. Pick the youngest leaves; older leaves are bitter, have an unpleasant texture and can act as a laxative, so are not recommended.

WHERE TO FIND: All too frequently nettles find you before you find them, alerting you to their presence with their powerful sting. They can be found on any nitrogen-rich soil

– nettles indicate good fertile land. Look around the garden for new clumps, in hedgerows or on patches of wasteland.

NETTLE SOUP

50g (2oz) butter
1 chopped onion
225g (8oz) potatoes, peeled and chopped
225g (8oz) young nettle leaves, washed and dried
2 tablespoons lovage or Alexander leaves
250ml (¼ pintt) milk
450ml (¾ pint) vegetable stock
Seasoning to taste

Heat the butter gently in a large pan, add the onion and cook until translucent. Add the potatoes, nettles and the lovage or Alexanders and allow to sweat on the heat for about 10 minutes. Add the milk and stock, bring to the boil and simmer for 15 minutes. Leave the soup to cool, then liquidise in a food processor. Return to the pan and heat gently before serving.

WATER MINT (*Mentha aquatica*)

If, like me, you are a mint aficionado and enjoy trying different varieties, you should keep an eye open for water mint. Water mint hybridises with spearmint (*Mentha spicata*) to produce the sterile peppermint. It can be used much as garden mint to make tea or as flavouring in fruit cups and sauces and has a very fine flavour. You could also try making a mint julep or a *mojito*.

DESCRIPTION: This perennial herb grows 15–90cm (6in–3ft) and spreads readily by creeping rhizomes. It has reddish

stems, toothed oval leaves and mauve flowers born in whorls
at the top of the stems from July to October.

SEASON: Pick leaves from April to October: use the youngest
as older leaves become rather bitter.

WHERE TO FIND: As the name suggests, in damp places, on
the banks of streams, rivers and lakes and in marshes.

MINT JULEP

1 teaspoon caster sugar
2 sprigs water mint
Soda water
3 tablespoons bourbon

Put the sugar in a tumbler with one sprig of mint and a
little soda water and mash to release the flavour of the mint.
Remove the mint and discard. Pour in the bourbon and more
soda water to taste. Add a sprig of mint for decoration.

MINT SAUCE

2 tablespoons chopped fresh mint
3 tablespoons wine vinegar

Chop the mint finely – it's very easy if you use scissors –
then add the wine vinegar and 3 tablespoons cold water and
mix. I used to chop the mint for my mother for years and
knew vinegar was added, but made the mistake of using malt
vinegar on my first solo attempt – the end result was truly
disgusting. It's important to use good wine vinegar.

WILD GARLIC (*Allium ursinum*)

Garlic has been used as a culinary flavouring for centuries and wild garlic, or ramsons, offers a subtly different, but equally delicious, taste experience. The leaves can be chopped into salads or slipped into sandwiches. The flowers taste delicious, look wonderful in a salad – and will impress guests at a dinner party. Richard Mabey's brilliant book *Food for Free* (see Bibliography, page 94) taught me that they were perfect mixed with tomatoes and I use them in a tomato salad with mozzarella and add them to fresh tomato sauce and pasta, for which I cannot thank him enough.

DESCRIPTION: Garlic is a bulbous perennial with broad, strong-smelling leaves like spears and white starry flowers. See right for illustration.

SEASON: The leaves appear from March onwards, flowers from April to June.

WHERE TO FIND: Wild garlic is naturalised throughout Europe and can be found on the fringes of woodland. It will colonise suitable areas and you can often smell it before you see it.

ROADKILL

The highway supermarket is a real test of our commitment to eating wild food. I can freely confess that although I eat meat with great relish, I have in the past baulked at the sight of my favourite delicacy complete with feathers, skin and a certain amount of blood. Interestingly, those who would usually avoid eating meat are quite happy to eat just this kind of fare, for this is an animal that has not been killed for food, but which, one hopes, has had many happy days right up to that last fatal decision to cross the road. In addition, they are not factory farmed and, with the exception of pheasants, are antibiotic free. Devotees maintain that they have saved many thousands of pounds over the years by eating from the wild larder.

In the United States and Australia roadkill is collected and eaten with far more enthusiasm and fewer qualms than in the United Kingdom. Some restaurants even offer the service 'from your grille to our grill'! In the United States it is estimated that one million birds and mammals are killed daily. The Mammals Trust UK, which keeps a tally of roadkill in the United Kingdom, believes that rabbits are the biggest mammal casualties with around 80,000 deaths a year. The badger, deer and grey squirrel populations each lose about 50,000 per year. The toll among pheasants is believed to be as high as 3,000,000 – that's an awful lot of potentially good meat going to waste. Legislation brought into force to outlaw badger baiting makes it illegal to have any part of the animal in your possession, but the law has not as yet been tested on roadkill. Other candidates for the table include hare, partridge, wild boar, hedgehog and blackbird.

In our plastic shrink-wrapped food environment most of us can no longer tell whether or not we can safely eat the meat we find. Most roadkill has been, effectively, killed by a blow, which produces a violent but quick end. In very many cases the meat will be of excellent quality and suitable for eating.

Obviously if the animal is warm and floppy it has been killed recently; rigor mortis will also indicate that the animal has not been dead for very long. However, rigor mortis reflects a transient period when the muscles start decaying very soon after death. The process is dependent on the temperature and can start within an hour of death or can be delayed for a few days in cold weather. It is important to bear in mind that all the meat we buy has been properly 'hung' so that the early stages of decomposition tenderise the meat. For all intents and purposes roadkill that has been dead for a few days is simply going through the same process.

After a few days many carcasses will become fly blown, where flies have laid their eggs and maggots have hatched and started to eat the meat. This can be a further indication that the meat is 'ripe' and as long as it is cleaned carefully, all maggots removed, and properly cooked it is safe to eat. In all the best stately homes the gamekeeper hangs up any catches intact and places a basket underneath: when the first maggots drop into the basket the meat is ready for the kitchen. Good food preparation relies on a combination of natural enzymatic digestion (rotting), followed by a cooking technique that ensures any unwanted organisms and micro-organisms are destroyed. Basic hygiene is also important to guard against

85

salmonella, wash all meat thoroughly, ideally in a separate area away from kitchen; small animals can be washed in sinks or bowls, larger animals can be washed in the bath. Particular care must be taken with badger meat which is prone to salmonella. All roadkill should be thoroughly cooked to eliminate bacteria and, in this instance, avoid rare steaks.

MAKING FURTHER CHECKS

It is possible that a roadkill animal may have crossed the road in a weakened state – it may have been ill or poisoned. If the carcass looks emaciated it is best to leave it, as this is an indication of ill-health – similarly if the skin is jaundiced or yellow, if the corpse smells rotten, or the eyes look dull and sunken it may have been sitting around for too long. However, if the animal looks plump and you can see evidence of trauma then you can reasonably assume that this was the cause of death. Fresh blood or feathers blowing around also indicate a recent fatality.

The trauma involved in a road accident can make shards of bone enter the muscles and this can be a nuisance when eating, but nothing more. If, however, you can see that any part of the digestive tract (gizzard) or the stomach and intestines are ruptured then toxins may have invaded the surrounding tissue – especially if the animal has been around for a few days – and this will make it taste unpleasant. If you get as far as taking the roadkill home – opening it up to remove the insides and discover a lot of green – this will indicate that the spleen has split and there is no point continuing for the meat will taste horrible. Foxes, which taste very good, rather like goat, can contain small fox tapeworm, a parasite which can cause echinococcosis, a potentially fatal infection. Humans more generally contract this illness from gardening without gloves, or failing to wash their hands when they have come into contact with fox, or indeed dog faeces.

Theoretically you can eat any roadkill you find. The one important rule to remember is that if you have run the animal over yourself, you are not allowed to collect it. It does seem a little bit of a shame; Emily, a friend of mine, hit a pheasant and, without realising it, drove all the way to work with the bird stuck to the front of her radiator. The car was badly damaged but poor, distraught, law-abiding Emily couldn't face taking the small consolation prize home for dinner.

You will doubtless come across other dead birds away from the roadside. If you can see a reason why they might have died – such as electric power cables overhead – it is again quite safe for you to consume them. You can be as daredevil as you like: a friend's father once tried seagull. It tasted disgusting apparently, although some maintain it is delicious – better than pheasant and goose-like in flavour. Squirrel, a once commonplace food, is said to be tasty. Elvis Presley reputedly ate it and it was traditional fare in rural Kentucky, the brains being considered a particular delicacy. However, research suggests that there may be links between cases of CJD and the consumption of squirrel brains as these contain the same kind of prions that are found in the soft tissues of cows and which can lead to Creutzfeldt-Jakob Disease. I have read mixed reports of badger, and have been cautioned that they are incredibly hard to skin and are best avoided during the breeding season (February to April) as the males tend to be musky smelling which makes for unpleasant tasting meat. The Protection of Badgers Act, 1992, makes it an offence to kill or take a badger, but there are exceptions; an injured badger can be taken to be treated by a vet and a seriously injured badger can killed as an act of mercy. Legalities aside be aware that some farmers still use illegal, banned substances, which can contain cyanide, to kill badgers. The bodies are then left at the side of the road to give the appearance of roadkill; the meat would be contaminated and dangerous to eat. As stated, the law has not yet been tested on roadkill with regard to badgers.

PHEASANT AND WOOD PIGEON

Some caution needs to be exercised when roadkill pheasant is found. Antibiotics are usually put into pheasant food, a practice which must be discontinued one month prior to the start of the season to render them safe to eat. Therefore the best time to eat roadkill pheasant is when it is in the four month shooting season; namely 1st October to 1st February in the UK or 1st October to 31st January in Northern Ireland.

Whether or not you choose to hang a pheasant is down to personal taste; the longer the meat is hung the stronger the flavour becomes. I do not personally enjoy the ripe flavour of a well-hung pheasant; I prefer the lighter, more chicken-like taste of a fresher bird. Try putting very fresh meat in a food processor to tenderise it and then use it for sausages. Preparing a bird for the kitchen is quite a simple task; if you get confused, examine a chicken in the supermarket and you will see clearly what needs to be done – the principles are the same, just the scale is different.

Firstly, open the legs and cut upwards from the vent until you have a large enough opening to put your hand in and pull out all the insides. Remove the head and the feet. You can pluck the bird: to do this pull the feathers out against the direction they lie in. This is a time-consuming business and it is much easier to skin the bird. Again, visualise a prepared chicken or turkey that you are about to stuff, ease the skin away from the tissue around the opening and then peel it back – all the feathers will come off with the skin and the job is done in a jiffy. The same technique applies to all birds.

Pigeon needs to have the breast wrapped in fat bacon or ham and be well coated in oil to prevent it drying out. It can then be stuffed and roasted exactly like a tiny chicken. Alternatively try pot roasting, half covering the bird with stock which keeps it moist and avoids the need for basting.

RABBIT

Rabbit is still for sale in any good butchers and really is delicious. Do pick one up when you see it on the side of the road, take it home and brace yourself to try the skinning process. You will find it much easier than you think: some men find it worryingly therapeutic – it is after all, what their ancestors did for many centuries. To prepare a rabbit cut it from the back legs to the top of the rib cage and remove all the insides, though you can pop the kidney and the liver back in to the body cavity to cook as they are considered to be delicacies. You must then remove the bladder gently – you don't want this to split or leak as the meat will spoil if urine is spilled on it. The next task is to skin the rabbit: to do this open up the bone that joins the rear legs together, then score around the joints that join the lower portion of the back legs together on each side. You then push the leg through, inside out, on each side and you follow this by pulling the skin off the rabbit. This is really quite easy to do as you are pulling against the tissue.

Some people cook rabbit heads to make brawn. A simple old-fashioned recipe for rabbits involves stuffing them with onions, a little garlic and parsley, and stewing them in stock with some red wine until the meat falls from the bone.

USEFUL ORGANISATIONS

ASSOCIATION OF BRITISH FUNGUS GROUPS (ABFG)
Harveys
Alston
Axminster
Devon EX13 7LG
www.abfg.org
The UK's leading voluntary fungus conservation body. ABFG members are all amateur enthusiasts and there are local groups across the country.

THE BOTANICAL SOCIETY OF THE BRITISH ISLES (BSBI)
41 Marlborough Road
Roath
Cardiff CF23 5BU
www.bsbi.org.uk
Information on the Code of Conduct on Wild Plants.

BRITISH MYCOLOGICAL SOCIETY
The Wolfson Wing
Jodrell Laboratory
Royal Botanic Gardens
Kew
Surrey TW9 3AB
www.britmycolsoc.org.uk
The sole objective of the BMS is to promote mycology (fungi) in all its aspects. The society holds meetings, issues publications and runs workshops and forays for field mycologists.

BRITISH PHYCOLOGICAL SOCIETY
www.brphycsoc.org
The British Phycological Society is a registered charity that aims to advance education by the encouragement and pursuit of all aspects of the study of algae (seaweed). Identification courses are run annually.

THE COUNTRYSIDE ACCESS AND ACTIVITIES NETWORK
The Stableyard
Barnett's Demesne
Belfast BT9 5PB
Northern Ireland
www.countrysiderecreation.com
CAAN is an umbrella organisation responsible for undertaking practical recreational strategies in Northern Ireland.

COUNTRYSIDE COUNCIL FOR WALES ENQUIRY SERVICE
Maes y Ffynnon
Penrhosgarnedd
Bangor
Gwynedd LL57 2DW
Wales
www.ccw.gov.uk
The CCW is the government's statutory advisor on sustaining natural beauty, wildlife and the opportunity for outdoor enjoyment in Wales and its inshore waters.

DEPARTMENT FOR ENVIRONMENT, FOOD AND RURAL AFFAIRS (DEFRA)
Customer Contact Unit
Eastbury House
30–34 Albert Embankment
London SE1 7TL
www.defra.gov.uk
UK Government department responsible for issues relating to the environment, food and rural affairs.

FERGUS THE FORAGER
Canterbury, Kent
www.wildmanwildfood.co.uk
Foraging and wild food cookery courses run from March to November. See website for information on the edible plants, seaweeds and fungi of the British Isles.

FIELD STUDIES COUNCIL
Montford Bridge
Preston Montford
Shrewsbury
Shropshire SY4 1HW
www.field-studies-council.org
The FSC is an environmental education charity committed to helping people to understand and be inspired by the natural world.

FORESTRY COMMISSION GB AND SCOTLAND
Silvan House
231 Corstorphine Road
Edinburgh
Scotland EH12 7AT
www.forestry.gov.uk
A government department for the protection and expansion of Britain's woodlands and forests.

JOINT NATURE CONSERVATION COMMITTEE (JNCC)
Monkstone House
City Road
Peterborough PE1 1JY
www.jncc.gov.uk
JNCC is the statutory advisor to the British government on UK and international nature conservation. It has information on the WCA Protection of Wild Plants and CRow.

MAMMALS TRUST UK
15 Cloisters House
8 Battersea Park Road
London SW8 4BG
www.mtuk.org
The Mammals Trust UK is a charity dedicated to the raising of funds to help conserve all UK native species and raise funds for scientific research.

NATURAL ENGLAND
1 East Parade
Sheffield S1 2ET
www.naturalengland.org.uk
*Natural England has been formed by
bringing together English nature, the
landscape, access and recreation
aspects of the Countryside Agency
and the environmental land-
management functions of the Rural
Development Service. The countryside
code can be found on the website:*
www.countryside.gov.uk

THE NATIONAL TRUST
Heelis
Kemble Drive
Swindon
Wiltshire SN2 2NA
www.nationaltrust.org.uk
*The National Trust is a charity
committed to preserving and opening to
the public many historic houses and
gardens. It also manages many
thousands hectares of forests, fens,
woods, rivers, downs and nature
reserves and hundreds of miles of
coastline for ever, for everyone.*

SCOTTISH NATIONAL HERITAGE
Great Glen House
Leachkin Road
Inverness IV3 8NW
Scotland
www.snh.org.uk
www.outdooraccess-scotland.com
*SNH works with Scotland's people to
care for the natural heritage, help
people to enjoy and value it and
encourage people to use it sustainably.*

THE WILDLIFE TRUSTS
The Kiln
Waterside
Mather Road
Newark
Nottinghamshire NG24 1WT
www.wildlifetrusts.org
*The Wildlife Trusts is a voluntary
organisation dedicated to conserving
the full range of the UK's habitat
and species.*

THE WOODLAND TRUST
Autumn Park
Dysart Road
Grantham
Lincolnshire NG31 6LL
www.woodland-trust.org.uk
*The Woodland Trust is the UK's
leading conservation charity dedicated
solely to the protection of our native
woodland heritage.*

BIBLIOGRAPHY

A Cook's Tour, Anthony Bourdain (Bloomsbury, 2002)

A Field Guide to the Crops of Britain and Europe, G.M. De Rougemont (Collins, 1989)

A Field Guide to the Trees of Britain and Northern Europe, Alan Mitchell (Collins, 1979)

Alternative Foods: A World Guide to Lesser-known Plants, James Sholto Douglas (Pelham Books, 1978)

An Omelette and a Glass of Wine, Elizabeth David (Penguin Books, 1985)

Food for Free, Richard Mabey (Collins, 2007)

Food from the Wild, Ian Burrows (New Holland, 2005)

Food from Your Garden (Reader's Digest, 1977)

Food in England, Dorothy Hartley (Little, Brown, 1999)

Good Housekeeping Herb Book: How to Grow and Cook with Herbs Successfully, Jane Eastoe (Harper Collins, 2002)

Grass Roots: The Universe of Home, Paul Gruchow (Milkweed Editions, 1995)

Mushrooms, Roger Phillips (Macmillan, 2006)

Plants for a Future: Edible and Useful Plants for a Healthier World, Ken Fern (Permanent Publications, 1997)

Ray Mears Outdoor Survival Handbook, Ray Mears (Ebury Press, 2001)

Seashore, Ken Preston-Mafham and Rod Preston-Mafham (Collins, 2004)

The Country Diary Herbal, Sarah Hollis (Henry Holt & Co., 1990)

The Growing Summer, Noel Streatfeild (Collins, 2000)

The Herb Book, Arabella Boxer and Philippa Back (Octopus Books Ltd, 1985)

The Magic Apple Tree: A Country Year, Susan Hill (Penguin Books, 1983)

The Outdoor Survival Manual, Garth Hattingh (New Holland Publishers Ltd, 2007)

The Wild Flowers of Britain and Northern Europe, Richard and Alastair Fitter (Collins, 1996)

Wild Flowers, Marilyn Jones (Kingfisher Books Ltd, 1980)

Wild Flowers in their Seasons, F. Edward Hulme (Cassell and Company Ltd, 1907)

AUTHOR'S ACKNOWLEDGEMENTS

A number of people have generously given of their time to assist me in writing this book. I would like to thank Graham and Derrick West, of West Whelks in Whitstable, Vic Chance, from Surnam the butchers in Tankerton, and our local vet, Roger Baker, who both ministers to our menagerie and proffers helpful advice. Warren Beesley from The Pearson's Arms in Whitstable kindly gave me his wonderful recipe for razor-shells; mine aren't quite as tasty as his yet, but with practice I aim to reach his heights of perfection. I must also thank my little helpers Florence, Teddy and Genevieve who pick and collect and who are game to try almost everything!

INDEX